BE
# Prepared
TO BE
## Lucky

*To Jim and Lois!*

# BE
# Prepared
## TO BE Lucky

Reflections on Fifty Years
of Public and Community Service

Paul S. Grogan and Kathryn E. Merchant

ORANGE *frazer* PRESS
*Wilmington, Ohio*

Published for the copyright holder by:
Orange Frazer Press
37½ West Main St.
P.O. Box 214
Wilmington, OH 45177

For price and shipping information, call: 937.382.3196
Or visit: www.orangefrazer.com

Book and cover design:
Orange Frazer Press with Catie South

Library of Congress Control Number: 2023924511

First Printing.

*To Lauren Louison Grogan,*
*our partner in bringing*
*this book to life.*

# Table of Contents

# Preface

Time and time again, throughout his progressively successful career as a civic leader spanning nearly fifty years, Paul Grogan has proven that actions speak louder than words—even louder than his own polished and inspiring prose!

Paul's career as a civic leader and change maker can be neatly divided into four segments: a decade working for two Boston mayors (Kevin White and Raymond Flynn) running point on key issues including community schools, neighborhood development, and jobs; thirteen years as CEO of LISC, the country's largest community development financial intermediary, during which time he published *Comeback Cities*; a three-year stint at Harvard University as vice president for government, community, and public affairs; and his career capstone, the two decades he served as president and CEO of the Boston Foundation, one of the most widely admired foundations in America.

An impressive biography indeed.

But underneath these credentials, propelling his success, lie the skills that unite Paul's leadership platform: founder, talent developer, relationship builder, collaborator, community advocate, institution transformer, boundary crosser, public speaker. And the scaffolding for this platform? A firm belief that an ounce of fate plus a pound of effort equals a ton of impact.

To some people, a reading of my words of introduction—this description of Paul's personal platform—could be just that: words. Popular words. Biography-speak. Civic sector jargon.

But please read on.

The themes and threads of Paul's career demonstrate the profound influence he has had on the fields of community development and community philanthropy. Life lessons drawn from fifty years of focus on changing community trajectories form the narrative and structure of this book.

I think his advice offers good reasons to read this book, regardless of whether you are thinking about going to college, graduating with an undergraduate degree ready to explore your first career step, or already focused with great intentionality on a career in public service.

*Be Prepared to Be Lucky* follows the arc of Paul's long career, creating a memoir that captures his recollections and stories amplified by interviews with twenty-seven colleagues. With their respective publishers' permission, we have incorporated excerpts from *Comeback Cities*, written with Tony Proscio in 2000, and the introduction to *The Good City: Writers Explore 21st Century Boston*, written in 2004, as well as selected media and other publications written by or about Paul and his work. In the final chapter, Paul's perspective on a career in public and community service offers food for thought, particularly for young civic leaders facing both familiar and new challenges in modern times. It is Paul's call to action, an open invitation to all young people who seek to make a difference in government, foundations, nonprofit organizations, and as community volunteers.

Paul Grogan was (and is) always prepared, and smart enough to know how lucky he was to seize opportunities when they came his way. Had this book been co-authored by another person, I would most certainly have sprinkled in my own story ingredients. Instead, I was lucky to co-author this book with Paul. We share a love for making a difference using the blend of community development with community philanthropy.

The Roman philosopher Seneca is credited with coining the phrase, "Luck is what happens when preparation meets opportunity." Enjoy Paul's journey and *Be Prepared to Be Lucky*.

With great admiration and gratitude,

Kathy Merchant

Cincinnati | October 2023

# Introduction

One of my favorite sayings is taken from E.B. White's famous quote, "No one should come to New York to live unless he is willing to be lucky." My take on that quote, which is now the name of this book, is *Be Prepared to Be Lucky*.

I particularly like this adaptation because it doesn't take sides on the things that influence us. Some people say that whatever happens, happens. Others are more optimistic that they can be captains of their own ships. In reality, a person's life ends up being a combination of those things, of fate and effort.

As I reflect on a career spanning nearly fifty years of community and public service devoted to cities, I may have worked for four different employers, but I've done the same job in every one of those places. You make each job into the one you want (if you're lucky). My early lessons in civic leadership have been repeated in a continuous thread throughout my career.

I deeply appreciate that my family background and upbringing provided opportunities and strong support to pursue my passion for making a difference in cities. It was fantastic preparation for a career in community and public service. Through various life experiences, I learned that, for me, a hands-on approach to public service would be most satisfying. While I recognize that every person's journey into public service will be different from mine, it is my hope that sharing my stories will align with readers' fundamental values of servant leadership.

I was born in Evanston, Illinois, to Robert S. Grogan, Jr., and Barbara Putzski Grogan. My father was a World War II combat veteran, graduate of

Paul Grogan #40 senior year basketball at Clinton High School.

Antioch College, and lifelong public school teacher and administrator. My mother was a graduate of Smith College. Both of my parents had strong commitments to public education. My mother particularly had strong expectations for well-mannered conduct and worthy accomplishments by my sisters, Janet and Sara, and me.

We moved around a lot within upstate New York for my father's various teaching and administrative posts—to Long Island, Cornwall on the Hudson, Corning, and then finally to Clinton. I actually hated all the moving, but those final three years at the public high school in Clinton where Dad was superintendent were really important to me. First of all, I was a very good basketball player in a town where all the best athletes played hockey, so I was able to break all kinds of records on the court!

More seriously, it was the mid-sixties and American cities were burning in protest for civil rights and against the War in Vietnam. From our bucolic town in upstate New York, they could have seemed distant events, but our family sat mesmerized in front of television network news every night. Dad and Mom were conservatives—they voted for Richard Nixon in 1960—but they realized that things were terribly broken in America around issues of race and they wanted to do something about it.

My parents' first action was to invite an Ethiopian high school student from the American Field Services Program to live with us during my junior year. I had never met, never mind befriended, a Black person. But the year that Magerssa Yadeca spent as my roommate, classmate, and friend were both wonderful and unforgettable. Some people in the town did not feel the same way, so I had my first introduction to the ugliness of racism.

My dad learned about the promise of a new program called "A Better Chance" (ABC) that brought inner city Black children to suburban communities to live with a family, attend high school, and hopefully receive a better-quality education. Colleague superintendents from around the country told him about its success and he decided to bring the ABC program to Clinton. He succeeded in placing two students in the program in Clinton before the school committee drove him from his job and shuttered the program. This experience foreshadowed the importance of race to me personally and remained a priority throughout my career.

In 1968, I was college bound—a tremendous piece of luck in that particular year. One of the many absurdities of the War in Vietnam was the

(Left to right) Senior pictures for Paul Grogan and Magerssa Yadeca.

gross unfairness of the draft deferral for college students. Some of my high school contemporaries in Clinton were not so lucky and lost their lives at a very young age serving their country. I never forgot that. At every high school reunion since, those who gathered have reflected on their luck and remembered those who never came home.

I could have stayed in Clinton to attend Hamilton College. By that point, however, I was ready to leave home, so I pursued early admission and was fortunate to attend Williams College. I loved the campus, and the community had a similar feel to Clinton—home away from home. It seemed like a school where one could be challenged academically, even without a clear roadmap toward a major. It is a small liberal arts college with a surprisingly robust sports program.

That turned out to be a lucky choice.

At the time, undergraduates were expected to master a certain body of knowledge in literature as a prerequisite to selecting a major. Like a lot of freshman students, I'd done very well in high school and was a particularly good writer, so I expected my college experience to be a seamless continuation. However, my first couple of English and history papers were absolutely decimated with devastating comments. I was certainly shocked at how unprepared I really was, but I worked hard to recover my confidence.

Happily for me, the next two years were full of wonderful experiences.

Sometimes you get lucky and people see things in you that you don't see in yourself. Two history professors took an interest in me and started pushing me to excel in various ways. That's part of the magic of a place like Williams College where small classes invite intellectual and social relationships with faculty. I decided to major in American Studies. My professors strongly encouraged me to write an honors thesis. I reluctantly followed their lead to write about the effects of immigration on compulsory education laws in American cities during 1880–1920, and how we Americans try to use schools to solve social problems. I was glad I did. My senior thesis was awarded the highest honors distinction, given to only four of sixty-plus American Civilization majors. That "first book" sparked my lifelong interest in and passion for education.

Another big impact on my time at Williams was the Civil Rights Movement happening in parallel to the War in Vietnam. Those issues had moved beyond our family's living room TV into the center stage of my life. Williams College was admitting significantly more African Americans. These students brought a heightened awareness of the Civil Rights Movement to Williams. There was a lot of unrest on campus. In fact, during our freshman year, one of the big events was the takeover of the administration building by the African American Student Union. The leader of that effort was Preston Washington, Jr., a senior at the college. I have never forgotten his electrifying address to the entire campus community in the fall of 1968. I would like to think that Preston's oratory prowess inspired me to hone my own public speaking skills. Ironically, thirty years later, Preston and I shared a podium to receive Williams College's highest honor, the Bi-Centennial Medal, for our work in reviving Harlem. But more on Harlem later in the book.

I got my first taste of the power behind being prepared *and* persuasive as the elected student member of the campus Committee on Educational Policy. I was invited to a faculty meeting to discuss a controversial proposal to dispense with grades in creative writing courses. We students felt this idea should be tried as a limited experiment in one area of the curriculum. As we thought about it at that time, we were sure this would not bring about the decline of western civilization! However, most of the faculty were dead set against it. Very unexpectedly, the committee chairman called on me to speak as a student representative. The setting in Griffin Hall was intimidating, a theater in the round two stories high surrounded by the entire faculty! Apparently, I was credible because my remarks turned the tide, and the proposal was approved. It was a heady experience, memorable and emblematic of the feeling that I just might have something going for myself.

After graduation from Williams College in 1972, I seriously considered an academic career as an historian but did not want to go immediately to graduate school. I thought a middle course that would allow me to at least make a living and consider this path more deeply would be to get a job teaching in a good high school.

There was a market for freshly minted graduates willing to work in private high schools for very little pay. I accepted an offer from the University School in Milwaukee where I taught history and English to juniors and seniors. I had family roots there. My father's parents were still alive at that point, living in West Bend right outside Milwaukee. A special dimension of my Wisconsin experience is that I was able to spend a significant amount of time with them. I think I was paid the princely sum of $6,500 for teaching four courses and coaching three sports. (Today that starting salary would be about $47,000.)

I ended up doing that teaching job for two years and had a terrifically important experience. It taught me that I was sufficiently ambivalent about an academic career to abandon the idea. I was hungry to be more directly involved in matters of urban revitalization. I ended up leaving Milwaukee after two years, moving to Boston, and joining city government. I went to work for another Williams graduate, Kevin White, who was the mayor of Boston at that time.

And that's where my story of devotion to public and community service begins. I hope this book inspires you to craft your own journey.

I want to express my gratitude to Lauren Louison Grogan who began this journey with me in 1981 as my chief of staff in the White administration. Our friendship and mutual interest in urban policy continued over the years and in 2018 we married. As in all things, she's been my partner and soulmate in writing this memoir.

In closing, I want to thank my co-author Kathy Merchant whose vision, talent, and determination made this memoir possible.

Paul Grogan

# Timeline of Paul's Career

**1968–1972** — **Williams College**
B.A. with highest honors in American History

**1972–1974** — **Secondary School Teacher**
The University School of Milwaukee, Wisconsin

**1975–1985** — **City of Boston**
Kevin White and Ray Flynn Administrations
   ≈   Director, Neighborhood Development and Employment
       Agency (1982–85)
   ≈   Deputy Director, Neighborhood Development and
       Employment Agency (1980–82)
   ≈   Director, The Boston Community School Program (1978–80)
   ≈   Special Assistant to the Mayor, City of Boston (1975–78)

**1979** — **Harvard University Graduate School of Education**
Masters' Degree in Education Administration

**1986–1998** — **Local Initiatives Support Corporation (LISC)**
President and CEO

**1997** — **Williams College Bicentennial Medal**
for leadership in inner-city revitalization efforts

**1999–2001** — **Harvard University**
Vice President for Government, Community, and Public Affairs

**2000** — *Comeback Cities*
co-authored with Tony Proscio

**2001–2021** — **The Boston Foundation**
President and CEO

BE
# Prepared
TO BE Lucky

# — 1 —

# Developing a Vision
# and Platform
# for City Vitality

1975–1985

My public career began in 1975 when I moved to Boston from Milwaukee. I came East because of relationships and because, as an undergraduate at Williams College, I had developed a serious interest in the history of education. I was very intrigued by how public schools were being used to solve some of the big problems in America. Boston was at the epicenter of this issue. School desegregation was playing out with particular force and difficulty in Boston.

I met my college friend and senior year roommate, Tom Howley, when we were eighteen. We were both drawn to music (and I was especially drawn to the quality of Tom's turntable). Although we have pursued different things and spent time in different geographic places, we've always been deeply connected in a way that is constant. We've had many conversations about things that really matter to us, things we're trying to figure out. We came out of the sixties, the Civil Rights Movement, Vietnam, and Watergate. Where was all this going? What makes for a meaningful life? Our shared sense of responsibility, decency, and obligation to make the world a better place grew strong roots in our youth. When we come back today to visit our friendship, that solidarity is still there.

Tom moved to Boston right after we graduated in 1972. Being from a politically active family in Cleveland, and having worked in Washington on summer college breaks, Tom wanted to dive directly into local politics.

3

One of our favorite stories is how Tom landed a job with Mayor Kevin White, a Williams College graduate, the dynamic young Boston mayor who was attracting a lot of attention nationally.

Tom's father was friends with George Steinbrenner—also a graduate of Williams College—who was at the time a prominent figure in Cleveland, owner of the New York Yankees, and chairman of fundraising for the Democratic National Committee. Mr. Howley petitioned Steinbrenner to gain leverage for his son to secure a job in Boston's White Administration. Apparently getting a modest request from a powerful donor was pretty much a no-brainer. Tom interviewed for a job on Kevin White's staff, got the job as an assistant speech writer to the mayor's chief of staff and speech writer, Ira Jackson, and gradually moved into bigger public roles organizing large events like Tall Ships, the Pope's first visit to Boston, and a convention of the U.S. Conference of Mayors. Tom proved to be very adept at organizing these events, and they helped move the needle on Boston's image as a world class city.

During the two years Tom was working in city hall, I was teaching high school in Milwaukee. I spent that time trying to figure out how to have a meaningful connection with people, teaching, and continuing to write about American history and education. Over the course of my conversations and correspondence with Tom, it became clear to both of us that I was eager (and ready) to have a more active role in civic life. I loved teaching, but at the time it wasn't as compelling as the notion of rolling up my sleeves to work in city administration.

Tom convinced me to come to Boston and be part of some exciting things going on in the city. I was keen to pursue an opportunity like Tom's position in the White Administration. My timing happened to coincide with the 1974 federal mandate to desegregate Boston Public Schools delivered by U. S. District Judge Arthur Garrity, Jr., which led to a busing crisis. My abiding interest in the history of public education led me to believe that it would be extraordinary to join the city administration as it worked through this issue.

Without having another job, I quit my teaching job in Milwaukee and moved to Boston. It took a few months to land a city position, so in the meantime, I knocked around doing odd jobs. At age twenty-four, I happily went to work in a very junior role in a policy research office, huddled in a tiny office with the mayor's chief of staff and speech writer, Ira Jackson. He was fond of telling me, tongue in cheek, that he had so much confidence in me that he resigned shortly after I arrived at city hall.

It was just six degrees of separation to say that George Steinbrenner—whom I never met—helped me get a job with the City of Boston and the White Administration. I would venture to say that everyone has a helpful connection somewhere within that "friend of a friend" chain. My advice is to be sure to look for the link and pursue it with vigor.

I thought it would be a brief interval in my early career, but I ended up staying in city government for ten years—with Mayor Kevin White for eight years (1975–83) and Mayor Ray Flynn for two years (1984–86)—initially as a junior staffer, but I was very soon positioned to help Mayor White craft and implement his vision of Boston becoming a world-class city. The mayor's ambition was neither self-evident nor guaranteed at the time, but I was excited to be a full participant in the work. Shortly thereafter, I was tapped to lead two successive city departments: community schools and neighborhood development. That final role, spanning both of the White and Flynn administrations, became what has since then been my life's interest and work: the revival of urban communities.

## Boston: A City in Crisis

I should begin this chapter with a snapshot of Boston as it was in the 1970s when the city was a full participant in the 20th century decline of urban America. Boston's story of decline, followed by a long period of renewal, became my story during the decade that I held increasingly responsible positions in city government. For my stories to resonate to a greater degree than snippets from my career, it is important to understand the social, economic, and political landscape in Boston at that time. Things were neither better nor worse in Boston than in other major cities, but it had become my city.

This reflection on Boston is an excerpt from the introduction I wrote for a 2004 collection of essays called *The Good City: Writers Explore 21ˢᵗ Century Boston*.

It is getting harder and harder to remember the bad old days, but they really weren't that long ago. The Harvard economist Edward Glaeser has written that "an urban observer looking at Boston in 1980 would have every reason to believe that it would go the way of Detroit and Syracuse and continue along its sad path towards urban irrelevance."

Just a few years before that, in 1975, Mayor Kevin White was dreaming up the renaissance of Faneuil Hall and Quincy Market, handsome but dilapidated eighteenth- and nineteenth-century buildings in the historic heart of the city. He and the legendary developer Jim Rouse were visiting every bank in town, trying to raise the financing. They got nowhere. In the dozens of polite meetings, the refrain they heard from Boston's captains of industry was, "This is a nice idea, but it will never fly."

This dismal view neatly summarized the profound pessimism about Boston at that time. Boston's own business leaders turned thumbs down, not on a project in a fringe neighborhood but on Faneuil Hall and Quincy Market, landmarks in the center of the city. Fortunately, Rouse and White got the money elsewhere, and the rest is history. We are even free, from today's lofty vantage point, to pooh-pooh the shops of Faneuil Hall Marketplace as, well, somewhat tacky and touristy. But the implausible success of this project began to make a very different statement about urban possibilities.

If, in 1975, Boston's downtown was emptied out and desolate, the city's neighborhoods were a train wreck: lunar landscapes of weed-filled vacant lots, boarded-up houses, and sidewalks carpeted with broken glass. The neighborhoods had been built to house almost 800,000 people, but by 1980 were home to only about 525,000—not nearly enough to keep things up. The massive exodus between 1950 and the 1990s was the fundamental underlying reality of the so-called urban crisis—the exit of people and value.

A great turn in Boston politics occurred in 1949, when the largely Irish Boston electorate turned away from the parochialism and ethnic polarization of James Michael Curley and his imitators and elected John Hynes mayor. Hynes talked of a "New Boston," embraced the largely Brahmin downtown business leadership, and launched the "urban renewal" period, which his successor John Collins brought into full flower.

Urban renewal is not remembered fondly today, and its products are legitimately despised by many. In Boston, urban renewal gave us a kind of rogues' gallery of design catastrophes: Charles River Park, City Hall Plaza, and the Prudential Center—preceded by the legendary demolitions of the West End and Scollay Square neighborhoods, places that are romanticized by today's urbanists as epitomizing the wonderfully messy genius of city life.

But the facile condemnation of this era from today's vantage point of revived urbanism fails to account for the true desperation of the 1950s and 1960s, a time when Boston was arguably dying. And urban renewal—crude, clumsy, and even anti-urban though it was—at least marked an attempt to stimulate investment, to build, to do something.

7

In an odd way, the mistakes of the period led us to smarter strategies in the days ahead: "Let's not do that again."

Like Hynes, White (narrowly elected for his first term as mayor in 1967) was the expansive, visionary alternative to a return to the cramped, parochial past, this time in the candidacy of Louise Day Hicks. Because of Faneuil Hall Marketplace, White is remembered as a great architect of Boston's downtown and waterfront revival, but his real genius was for the neighborhoods.

Boston is an innovative city, with a long list of civic "firsts" on its resume—the first public school, the first free public library, the first paid police force, and the first American subway. In his essay in *The Good City*, Scott Kirsner dubs Boston "Innovation City," and rightly so, because this city always has been a wellspring of technological firsts—from advances in electricity to general anesthesia to robotics. Kevin White initiated his own electrifying period of innovation, including the creation of "little city halls" in every neighborhood, "community" schools—which opened new school buildings for community use into the evening hours—and neighborhood health centers, a new kind of clinic that replaced the disappearing primary care physician. Energetic and charismatic, he recruited talented aides and defiantly promoted the "livable city" as a positive ideal.

Race is often the asterisk in accounts of Boston's progress, and the school desegregation crisis of the 1970s is still an uncomfortable defining moment for a city struggling to move beyond it. The drama of this era is actually what first enticed me to Boston, and into the Kevin White administration.

In America, we have routinely called upon our public schools to take on all of society's unsolved problems. We asked the schools to forge our democracy in the late eighteenth and early nineteenth centuries. Later, we asked them to assimilate the torrent of immigrants pouring into U.S. factories and farms. In the mid-twentieth century we asked them to win the cold war by turning out scientists, engineers, and mathematicians. And then in Boston, and in other cities, we asked them to cure the poisonous legacy of racial discrimination.

However justified the federal court finding that the Boston School Committee had systematically discriminated against Black schoolchildren, which it certainly had, the remedy of school busing to achieve racial balance delivered another great body blow to a city already reeling, hemorrhaging people and vitality to the suburbs and beyond.

## The Kevin White School of Management

Kevin White was larger than life for all of us who felt that cities were the moral cause of our generation. Mayors like Kevin had revolutionized the cause for cities to be rebuilt or saved. The city was suddenly a magnet for talent, the new frontier for courageous and ambitious people who wanted to change the world through the public sector. We were a throng of twenty-somethings, drawn to his passion and defiant optimism, eager to fight for his vision of a "world-class" Boston, certain we were doing something of great consequence. White wasn't going to let Boston become a second-rate city.

Mayor White surrounded himself with talented people who in some ways were smarter than he was. That has had a profound impact on me. I picked that out as a fundamental insight about how to get organizations to perform at a higher level.

Kevin was brilliant, but he could be brutal. If you had even a small lapse of not being brilliant around him, he eviscerated you. We used to say, "The mayor's appreciation is a highly perishable commodity."

> "If nobody's mad at you, you're not doing anything important.
>
> —Kevin H. White, former Mayor of Boston

I was in one meeting with the mayor and about half a dozen top people. I forget exactly what we were discussing. But at some point during the meeting there was a pause and I offered an observation about what was happening. The mayor drew himself back, looking at me with this slight shake of his head and said, "Paul, get in the game. You're sitting there with your football helmet on, and we're playing baseball." Imagine, there I was, twenty-six years old, and the mayor of Boston just said, 'get in the game.' That was tough but it reminded me of the serious business of running a billion-dollar corporation like the City of Boston.

Another lesson I learned from Mayor White in those early years: unless you can "sell" internally as well as externally, you cannot move an organization or a city. A big factor in that was his defiant optimism.

To counter negative publicity about busing and urban blight, the mayor initiated a sophisticated communications plan to create "tables" designed to bring together business, civic, and community leaders to discuss future opportunities for Boston. The mayor asked me to create a series of dinners offering leaders the opportunity for off-the-record conversations with each other, the mayor, and his top administrators. From those dinners sprang a prestigious award program branded "Grand Bostonians" honoring exceptional leaders of every race from every neighborhood and sector.

The mayor loved the program because it sent a strong message that Boston, despite its challenges, was a great city with extraordinary leaders all pulling in the same direction. I loved it because I made lifelong connections with community, business, academic, and media leaders. The Grand Bostonians program continues today under the auspices of the Greater Boston Chamber of Commerce and is one of the greatest honors Boston

"To Paul—for whose prose and patience I'm grateful. Kevin H. White." Grand Bostonian Awards at Parkman House, circa 1978.

bestows on its civic leaders. (I was honored to be named a Grand Bostonian in 2021.)

If you hung around long enough, you got asked to do things, to take on leadership roles, that went way beyond your qualifications on paper.

One of many important and lasting initiatives that I worked on at the time was authoring the city's original linkage report. Linkage was an idea conceived by then-City Councillor Bruce Bolling. Our 1978 report recommended imposing a tax on major development projects that would be used to fund affordable housing in Boston's neighborhoods. A Boston Redevelopment Authority study in 2000 analyzing the impact of ten similar statutory linkage programs in the United States found that Boston's linkage program was the most successful in the country. Success was defined as raising significant funds for affordable housing creation while at the same time encouraging economic growth and development. Today, Boston's linkage program continues under the moniker Development Impact Project, and since 1986 (when the linkage program was finally approved) has awarded $247 million for 297 projects resulting in 9,300 new affordable units of housing and preservation of 6,153 affordable units.

There was an unending stream of opportunities like this, of being flexible to step up and take charge of things where there was no assigned responsibility. For me it represented a continuing seminar on urban affairs. I would make the case to anyone considering joining a city administration or a mayor's staff to just do it. You will get responsibilities and make connections that will open all kinds of doors in your career, far beyond what you would likely experience in the private sector.

## Desegregation, Busing, and Carson Beach

Kevin White's conception of the desegregation and busing order was that his first responsibility was to hold the city together and not have the city destroyed by conflict. "The middle period of Kevin White's sixteen years as mayor was thoroughly preoccupied with getting the city through the trauma [of desegregation]. It was a scary period, in part because it licensed extremists and haters."[1]

What Kevin was so enraged about—and it was directed at U.S. District Court Judge Arthur Garrity—was that the Judge had a lot of flexibility to moderate the conflict by implementing the plan gradually, to not force busing and incite the ensuing violence. But Garrity imposed a citywide plan for desegregating Boston without the city's significant participation in the plan. Kevin was very upset about that. He felt it was completely unnecessary. This made a tough situation worse.

There were racial tensions all around the city which eventually led to some pretty severe community disturbances in one area called Carson

Beach, a Commonwealth of Massachusetts-owned public park right on the Black-White racial line between South Boston and Dorchester neighborhoods in the city.

On August 10, 1975, hundreds of Black protesters rallied at Carson Beach to assert their right to use Boston's public spaces. They were fed up with the indignity and terror of living in an intensely segregated city, all of which was exacerbated by school desegregation orders. The gathering started out as a peaceful protest, but quickly escalated into violence between Black and White demonstrators. It was an ugly situation that went on for the better part of a week before things calmed down. Boston was already suffering from a negative national reputation on racial rancor. This incident further cemented that perception.

As a very young, inexperienced person, new to City Hall, I was thrust into this situation as one of the mayor's representatives at Carson Beach long before I was ready for so much responsibility. The opportunity to take on enormous challenges, ready or not, was one of the tremendous benefits of public service then and remains so today.

Nothing in my upbringing in upstate New York or rural Massachusetts prepared me for the ugliness and violence of those times. My view was that the mayor should have been there in the early hours and days of the disturbances. But instead, there I was at Carson Beach as part of the staff group that was monitoring the situation, trying to advise the mayor on what we should do. Back in city hall, during a discussion to form a plan that wasn't crystallizing, the mayor looked at us—particularly at me—and said, "You can't advise me." It was said with a real 'you've got to be kidding' attitude, 'you're not going to be able to help me with this.' It was upsetting, for sure. However, he continued to rely on me as his point person.

I quickly gained a reputation for being calm and measured. Both the Black and White communities as well as the police department saw me as even-handed. I learned a lot about listening to the community, treating people with honesty and respect, and expecting the best, not the worst, from people. I carried that with me throughout my career. This lesson

Carson Beach in 1975. © *Boston Globe.*

prepared me to be lucky in more than one contentious community meeting over the years.

The mayor's eventual appearance was tardy by some estimates, including mine. When he arrived at Carson Beach, the whole situation changed as people gathered around him and the mayor called upon various people to speak. It completely changed the tone of the event, moderating the open hostility. Instead, there was palpable fascination with "the mayor's here." He had tremendous caché. He took a walk on the beach with some kids, gave them a chat about the importance of public spaces. As he walked along with his trademark jacket slung over his shoulder, it completely defused the situation. He had a tremendous ability to do that even when people were disappointed in him.

Later the mayor and I reviewed the events on Carson Beach. He told me he believed that his restraint was an example of how mayoral leadership should be deployed for maximum effect. In contrast with Kevin's approach, I learned years later that a young city councillor named Ray Flynn had set up a free public BBQ less than a mile away from Carson Beach in South Boston. His goal was to pull White kids away from joining the mob on the beach. This was clearly an example of using grassroots political capital by throwing yourself into the heart of the community, a practice Ray would continue with tremendous effect as mayor when he succeeded Kevin White.

One night I'll never forget, the mayor agreed to go over to East Boston for a community meeting about the controversial Logan Airport expansion. As it turned out, what was really happening was a big organizing effort by the anti-busing people. When Kevin got to the event at the high school auditorium, it was jammed with a howling mob. I didn't usually do advance work for community meetings, but there I was with the local police captain. We both told the mayor that this meeting had to be postponed because we couldn't guarantee his safety.

The mayor looked at the officer and said, "I can't wait," and he bounded up the stairs onto the auditorium stage. It was one of these stages where a middle "tongue" protruded into the audience. If you went to the end, you were surrounded on three sides. The screaming and howling continued, but Mayor White walked right to the end of the stage and just stood there with his hands on his hips and a big smile on his face. Finally—I don't know how long it was, but it seemed to be forever—the crowd began to quiet, and he had his meeting. It was quite impressive.

Boston's judicial desegregation and busing issues were not resolved officially until 1988. During that time, issues of race permeated the entire city. Years later, I wrote about a personal experience that affected me deeply:

Anyone who was [living in Boston] then had their own encounters with the unleashed bigotry and violence of the time. Mine was on a snowy night in 1977. My roommate and I were settled in, watching the late TV news in our triple-decker apartment in the Jamaica Plain neighborhood when we heard a frightful commotion outside... shouting, then screaming and crashing.

We hurtled down the stairs and onto the street where we interrupted four White men who were administering a merciless beating to a defenseless Black man who was already covered in blood. Well, we *thought* he was defenseless. Startled by our sudden arrival, the four thugs jumped into their idling white sedan and drove off. The victim pursued his attackers, grabbing a folding chair that was "reserving" a shoveled-out parking space on the narrow street (a Boston custom) and smashing it against the rear of the car, shattering a window in the process. We all gave chase, but the car, whose driver doused the lights so we couldn't read the license plate, vanished into the night. The beaten man, a Jamaican immigrant, had lost his coat in the scuffle and his white shirt was crimson. The good news was that he was not seriously injured, even though his facial cuts had bled profusely. He said, "You saved my life." I responded, "Man, you saved your own life."

Because my roommate and I both worked in the mayor's office, the next day we put our "access" to work. At our behest, the police department assigned a couple of detectives to the case. They shrewdly canvassed every auto glass shop in Boston, and by the end of the day they had made several arrests. It was my first experience with having some clout and I admit I liked it quite a lot.[2]

Another important lesson I learned during that contentious time is that courage matters. It can change the odds, as it did for that young Black man in my neighborhood.

## Jumping on the Fast Track

Several months into my tenure, Ira Jackson left the city to become an associate dean at Harvard's Kennedy School of Government, leaving no one to do Mayor White's speech writing at a critical juncture. Mayor White had been invited to make the keynote address at the 1976 National Urban League conference in Cleveland. Of course, the League was one of the leading civil rights organizations in the country at a time when Boston was being portrayed nationally in a very unflattering light on racial issues, particularly school desegregation and busing.

The speech quickly acquired tremendous importance as the mayor was quietly exploring a run for vice president of the United States. The deputy mayor came into my office, handed me something that couldn't even be considered a rough draft, and said "You've got to prepare this speech which is going to take place in a couple of weeks."

I was the new kid, so I didn't see much choice but to put together a draft for the mayor.

He sat on it for a few days and then summoned me into his office. I have never been so terrified in my life. I could have viewed it as an incredible opportunity, but at the time, that was the furthest thing from my mind.

Paul Grogan "jumping on the fast track" at City Hall!

I was focused on survival. That initial meeting went fine. But then I was summoned again, this time to the mayor's office at the Parkman House, an imposing mansion on Beacon Hill. He said to me, "Paul, I'm finding that I don't know if this is a good speech or a bad speech. I thought that one of the ways I could get more comfortable with this speech is if I actually heard it delivered, and that's what I want you to do now." So, stifling my fear, that's what I did. At the conclusion, the mayor just nodded and said, "See you later."

As it turned out, Mayor White decided to use the speech after vetting it with Samuel Huntington, then a prominent political scientist at Harvard. Sam liked the speech and encouraged the mayor to deliver it, which he did word-for-word. I heard from friends in Cleveland that the speech couldn't have gone better; in fact, it got a standing ovation.

Several days later, I was summoned to Mayor White's office once again. I'm thinking "take me to the top." At first, he ignored me while chatting with other people wandering in and out of his office. Finally, he looked over at me sitting on the couch and said, "Paul, we got a tremendous response. People absolutely loved the speech. They said, 'Mayor, that was a great speech. The *content* wasn't much, but the *delivery* was spectacular.'" I think that was his way of keeping me in check, making sure I didn't get too full of myself because of one great speech.

And that is how I became Mayor White's speech writer! Preparation met luck and opportunity head-on resulting in a perfect storm.

I kept a copy of that Urban League speech which is archived along with other important documents from the years that Kevin White served as mayor of Boston.[3] Nearly fifty years later, I am struck by how far we've come in addressing issues of race and equity in our country, yet how much more there is to do as we address another wave of challenges in the 21st century.

Mayor White's keynote address at the Urban League's 1976 annual conference was somewhat long and was meant to be spoken with emphasis rather than read, so I have chosen just a few salient excerpts to share in this chapter about the role of city government in addressing Boston's race and education issues.

Whether a municipal job is your first or forever career stop, it is my hope that the sentiments expressed in this abbreviated piece will resonate:

I believe that school desegregation creates a great dilemma for those of us who care about the health of our cities. But we can't begin to understand the dilemma until we grasp the fundamental political and social mood of the nation. Because without question that climate is profoundly affecting the progress of the entire civil rights movement in the 1970s.

That atmosphere—that climate—is not reassuring. In fact, it is profoundly disturbing. As a nation, we seem possessed by political pessimism, social nihilism, and economic fatalism, in danger of accepting that what we have is the best we can hope for. Taken together, these trends can deal a death blow to the continued pursuit of economic and social justice.

Recent events undermine our faith in government. An effective campaign is being waged to convince us that government can do little to solve our most pressing problems.

It makes me think we have very short memories. It is true that government hasn't solved all our problems. But as Al Smith [former governor of New York] used to say, let's look at the record. The intervention of government ended the Depression. The enlargement of government brought Social Security and unemployment compensation. The expansion of government opened Southern universities to Black students. And the involvement of government passed civil rights legislation in the 1960s.

We are all better off for these achievements. Enlarged government has generally expressed concern and compassion, and impatience with inequality and injustice. Black Americans made great strides during periods of activist government. At the end of the 1960s, Blacks were better housed, better educated, better employed, and better represented in government, than ever before.

As far-reaching as the changes of the sixties were, they were just a beginning, only the first hesitant and long-overdue steps. Statistics aren't needed to show us the blighted lives and blasted hopes of countless inner-city residents. In Cleveland and in Boston, it's the same: not just abandoned housing, but abandoned people, and not just unequal opportunity, but no opportunity at all.

It is in this context, in this rather dim light, that we see the controversial and conflict-ridden issue of school desegregation. I am well aware of the risks of broaching this subject. As mayor of a city convulsed by a busing order, I can testify to the passion it arouses, passions often beyond the recall of reason. A national debate is raging about the methods of school desegregation. It is critical to remember that, though busing has become a national issue, it is very much a local problem. What is true for one city may be irrelevant for another. Boston has its own demography, economy, and school system, as do Cleveland, Detroit, Denver, and so on.

I believe that Boston's experience holds some insights for Cleveland. Let me sum up our situation [in five key points]: (1) Busing in Boston was the result of the political and moral default of our School Committee. For years, deliberate policies isolated and restricted minority students. (2) At no point, during or after the court case, did the School Committee agree to cooperate. They denied their own misdeeds and vowed resistance. (3) The energy of much of the White working class went into organized opposition to the Court order. (4) In the face of political and popular intransigence, the role of the [federal] judge expanded enormously. The judiciary is neither fitted nor intended for this task. (5) After fully one and a half years of extensive busing to achieve racial balance, 85% of our public schools fail to meet court-established racial guidelines.

How is this possible? Simply stated, the White students aren't there. 17,000 of them are gone, out of the city, into parochial schools and private academies, or roaming the streets.

Boston and Cleveland have shared the maladies of our older cities: the debilitating exodus of jobs and people to the suburbs depriving us of revenue, destroying our neighborhoods, and threatening our very existence. The task of the seventies is to stem that flow, revive our communities, and restore faith in the urban future.

Can anyone ask the Black children of this country to wait till a better solution is found? An easier way to erase school discrimination? Of course not. We are left, then, with two choices. The first is to maintain our present course and risk white flight, institutional disruption, and urban decline. The second and more sensible alternative: pursue equal educational opportunity, yes, but don't destroy our cities in the process.

How might this be achieved? I think the political process—whatever its present disrepute—offers some guidelines. Politics, as everyone knows, is the art of the possible. Politics means compromise. And politics means the resolution of competing claims.

[In Cleveland] you have the opportunity...to exercise the courage, the creativity, and the compassion we could not—an opportunity provided by politics. Don't wait for the verdict of the court to affirm a position of conciliation and tolerance. Political polarization can be reduced by leaders with foresight and integrity. But one school committee member, or one city councillor, or one mayor, can't do it alone. The school system may be on trial in that courtroom, but the city of Cleveland is at stake.

If there is one lesson—one insight—worth remembering about busing in Boston, it is this: the leadership failed. They weren't up to it. At the community level, at the neighborhood level, at the precinct level, the leadership broke and ran. They couldn't stand the heat, the volatility, the explosiveness of the issue. It was not their finest hour.

If this country is going to solve its most pressing problems and fulfill its grandest ideals; if we are going to learn as a nation to eradicate poverty, to provide opportunity, to build decent housing, to educate our children; and if Black people and White people are going to learn to live, work, and grow together; it will be in the cities that these achievements are made.

If we lose those cities, we lose that vision of a better future for the generations that follow us.

## Creating Sustainable Public-Private Partnerships

Like Mayor John Hynes before him, Kevin White recognized the importance of the business community's capital, both financial and civic, and he made me his staff point-person on these efforts—a bit of luck that would hold me in good stead for every subsequent position I held in my career.

It was my instinct to build relationships even when I didn't have a specific purpose necessarily in mind. I would go beyond the usual suspects to bring people into a process who had different points of view. We didn't call it being a "boundary crosser" at the time, but that's a good way to put it in today's terms. Eventually I was on a short list of people who were equally welcome and well-known in both neighborhoods and corporate boardrooms.

I was fortunate early in my career at the City of Boston to be assigned to staff the creation of the Boston Private Industry Council (PIC). The PIC was created in 1979 by Mayor Kevin White and State Street Bank Chairman Bill Edgerly. It was the first organization in the nation designed to deliver federal job training resources and to engage private sector employers. The mission of the Boston PIC was and is to strengthen Boston's communities and its workforce by connecting youth and adults with education and employment opportunities that align with the needs of area employers.

In 1982, this new business-led model was legislated nationally. It was renewed as part of the Clinton Administration's 1998 Workforce Investment Act and again in 2014 (Workforce Innovation and Opportunity Act).

(Left to right) PIC 1982 Annual Meeting: Governor-elect Michael Dukakis, State Street Bank President Bill Edgerly, Mayor Kevin White, Federal Reserve Bank President Frank Morris, NDEA Director Paul Grogan, PIC Executive Director Cay Stratton, and John Hancock Insurance Company Chairman John McElwee.

Also in 1982, the PIC added summer jobs to its portfolio as part of the groundbreaking Boston Compact, an innovative school improvement agreement forged by business and higher education leaders with Boston Public Schools. The PIC launched the private sector component for summer jobs as part of the business commitment to the school system. A re-energized Boston Compact (2011) continues to provide a table for collaboration to break down traditional barriers between district, charter, and Catholic schools, and to prioritize student learning.

The Boston Housing Partnership (now called Metro Housing Boston) was another important initiative. BHP took the jobs program model of getting the private sector more involved and applied it to affordable housing. That's another great organization that is still going and shows no sign of

> Public-private partnerships were defined in Boston, invented in Boston, and redefined Boston.
>
> —Micho Spring, former Boston Deputy Mayor

flagging. There was something in the water in Boston during this period that allowed these partnerships to happen. It is still a badge of honor for the city that these kinds of entities have had such a long tenure.

The enduring magic of these public/private partnerships is that they give corporate leaders a ringside seat to understand the complex challenges of managing city government and a platform to do something about improving the quality of urban life. Perhaps the best example during my tenure in Boston city government is State Street Bank CEO Bill Edgerly, a tremendous corporate leader who exercised significant influence in all three of the partnerships I just described. Bill was the founding chair of the PIC and subsequently the Boston Compact. In both situations he came into close contact with Boston Public School students and was dismayed to learn about their deplorable housing conditions. In direct response, he convened a group of business leaders to help him create the Boston Housing Partnership. Today, the CEO of what is now called the State Street Corporation continues to play a significant role in the civic life in Boston.

A final example of public/private partnerships is the Main Streets Program. Tom Menino, who eventually became Mayor, was a very important person for me during the time he was a member of city council. Menino had been a top aide to a fellow named Joe Timilty, Kevin White's opponent in the previous election. This was an issue which was "very Boston": who you sided with in the previous election had a lot to do with what opportunity you had after the election. In those days, Boston was a payback city.

Nonetheless, Tom Menino and I hit it off. Unlike many of his fellow members of City Council at the time, Menino had good ideas and wanted to get something done, so I cultivated a strong working relationship with him. I met with him often on the budget when he chaired that committee. We forged a partnership when nobody else in the White Administration did that. Menino was very interested in neighborhood commercial districts which were in terrible shape—lots of boarded up storefronts, high crime rates, all typical of declining neighborhoods. He and I went to Washington D.C. together to meet with the National Trust for Historic Preservation to discuss the Main Street program, which at the time had no urban presence, and subsequently created Boston Main Streets. Many of these revitalized commercial districts still thrive to this day.

There is a direct connection in later years between our early foundation of good relationships and our working together on town/gown issues at the turn of the century when Menino was mayor and I worked for Harvard University.

# — 2 —

# Stepping Up
# to Leadership

Over the next decade, I was asked to turn around two troubled city agencies, starting with the Boston Community Schools. This particular set of battles was when I really began to understand the power of leadership in elevating community and what happens when it comes into conflict with the political machine.

After spending a few years doing policy work and speech writing, I felt ready to run something. One of the things that Kevin White did for a lot of people working for him was to give them that opportunity. "Be on my staff, do the scut work for a couple of years, and I'll give you a bigger opportunity down the road." That happened to me. And, to make the case for public service, my experience wasn't unusual.

### Leadership, Ethics & Opportunity | Take One
### Boston Community Schools (1978)

The Boston Community Schools program, a Kevin White innovation in 1972, was a network of public schools that had been declared community schools and opened to the public through the evening hours to help keep

> It takes confident leadership to develop trust so that people will join you in efforts to propel the work forward. It takes a leader that has a strong vision for a better community to be able to influence people, bring them together, be a collaborator. The three key character-based actions are listen, communicate, and engage.
>
> —Vanessa Calderón-Rosado, president of IBA

kids off the streets. The old settlement house idea of the 19th century, created to have school-based social services to help an influx of immigrants, was modernized when a bunch of new schools were built, many with swimming pools and nice athletic equipment. But Kevin White didn't want the Boston School Committee—a corrupt entity—to get control of these exciting new community schools. There was a battle which went on for a number of years between the community schools and city hall.

The community schools all had local boards with programmatic authority. It was one of the earliest attempts to distribute responsibility for what had been bureaucratic tasks. The problem with the local boards was that, in many cases, they started to use their positions to try to damage the mayor politically. The mayor was so enraged by the behavior of some of the community schools that he wanted to abolish the program. But before taking such a forceful step, he gave me the opportunity to run the Community Schools starting in 1978.

Although I was the CEO, I had very little authority—not the same level of authority as a city department head. It was a tremendous exercise in learning how to work with people, dealing with hostility and antagonism, using the power of *influence* rather than authority. That has served me very well in the rest of my career, knowing that you can't order anybody to do anything and expect flawless execution.

After a year or so, the Community Schools were working very well. I had restructured the program and hired an amazing crew of staff, many of whom were later tapped by the Flynn Administration for various department

head positions. I had learned
the lesson from Kevin White to
hire smart people and let them
do great work. These were good
people who could identify with
and relate to the community.
They had credibility, and they
were hard workers.

In 1981, the mayor gave me
the opportunity to be COO of
a much larger city agency, the
Neighborhood Development &

Boston Mayor Kevin White, Second Lady
Barbara Bush, and Paul Grogan, Director
of the NDEA; 1983.

Employment Agency (Boston) (NDEA). At the point I was leaving Community Schools to go to NDEA, I thought everything was fine. The next thing I heard, Mayor White had proposed shutting Community Schools down, not because of poor performance, but to save money. This was happening to many different city departments at the time under the guise of budget constraints but was mostly politically motivated. I couldn't believe it! He had never mentioned this idea to me when he was courting me for a c-suite position at NDEA.

I couldn't let the mayor use a budget gap as an excuse to eliminate the Community Schools program, so I cut staff and identified new sources of outside funding. One key source was a state funding program for adult literacy which garnered national attention (from Barbara Bush while her husband was Vice President) as well as program resources.

While I continued to argue with the mayor about saving the program, I started an internal campaign, going around to all the department heads, making the case for Community Schools and enlisting people to get concerned about the issue. Because this program was so important and deserving, as well as highly regarded, we wanted to defend it. It shouldn't be abolished.

To this day, I don't quite know why Kevin let me do this. He had to be aware of what I was doing—you could look at this as pure insubordination. I think he was amused by me in some way.

"Paul, I am trying to express myself without the aid of one of your speeches—my subject matter did not seem to impress you—but you have always impressed me." Mayor Kevin White, Thompson Island staff retreat, circa 1980.

The situation came to a head during a senior staff retreat at Thompson Island, where the Mayor and I had a chance encounter. We argued about the fate of Community Schools. I guess I won the argument because the Community Schools are still there today, stronger than ever.

## Leadership, Ethics & Opportunity | Take Two
## Neighborhood Development and Employment Agency (1982)

Like so many young people, I'd fallen in love with the idea of going to a great business school. In 1982, I decided to apply to both Stanford and Harvard.

As I reflect on these words from my application to Stanford some forty years later, and think about the way my professional career unfolded. I recognize these words as consistent elements of my personal and professional platform:

> My seven years of experience in city government has been a crucial testing ground of character and personal integrity, and also a time in which I became fundamentally committed to management as a career. Even before that, my college experience encouraged me to hone my communications skills and certainly formed habits of mind that I will have for a lifetime. The thoroughness with which I approach organizational problems, and the value I attach to the ability to articulate and persuade, are evidence of the influence of that period.

> I think I have emerged from my years in government with a reputation as this kind of a person—one with tenacity, skill, and a sound and steady moral compass—and I look upon it as an important accomplishment but also as an extremely formative and influential set of experiences. As director for the Boston Community Schools Program, my formal powers were so few that I had to build trust, and then persuade and cajole rather than impose by fiat.

> I take great pride in my ability to work with a wide variety of people…I am equally at home talking with a group of bank and insurance company heads as discussing a community issue with a civic association in a neighborhood meeting. I have a reputation for getting people to perform beyond what they believed to be their capacities and for successfully building teams within an organization. Two keys to these abilities are that I don't ask any more of anyone than I ask of myself, and that I am extremely loyal to members of my teams. Successful working relationships in organizational life depend heavily on mutual respect.

I was accepted at both universities. I decided on Stanford, confirmed I was coming to California that Fall, and I was nearly out the door. There was even a going away party for me.

But the situation in the White Administration's bureaucracy, specifically the relatively new NDEA, was getting worse by the minute.

It was about to burst into the open on the front page of the *Boston Globe*. It got ugly fast. The federal Department of Housing and Urban Development (HUD) started an investigation into the agency's administration of grants. Relations were so bad between HUD and the mayor's office that word leaked into the newspapers, which was very embarrassing for the mayor.

At that time, the Boston office of HUD included all of Massachusetts. HUD was a partner with other cities in Massachusetts, but in Boston the partnership had devolved into a regulatory situation. The city of Boston was in distress in the early 1980s, not only due to its overall economic condition, but also due to poor administration of federal Community Development Block Grant programs. Marvin Siflinger was the director of the Boston office at the time. He made very clear that no real progress was being made in fair housing or economic development initiatives funded by HUD, putting future funding in jeopardy. Block grant funding was cut in half.

The mayor called me to say that he really needed my help to fix the situation by staying on at NDEA and assuming the role of CEO. He offered to talk to the Stanford Dean himself, if necessary, to ask for a one-year deferral.

I really could not turn down Mayor White's plea for help given all that he had done for me, and the opportunities I had been given. I never got to Stanford, and I'm wistful about that. I do wish that I'd somehow been able to fit business school in with everything else. But perhaps that was lucky.

When I became the director of the NDEA, I called on the biggest CEOs. They didn't know why I was there, but they were very polite to receive me. I just said, "I want you to be aware of what we're doing and hear any thoughts or recommendations that you have."

There were a couple of very senior people in the administration who traditionally had a role in allocating the federal Community Development Block Grant and CETA employment and training funds that came into the city. They expected to continue to do that even as I came into my new role as head of the Agency with a mandate to clean things up because there were a lot of patronage dollars at stake.

I could see that they were making moves to control things. But I disabused them of that notion pretty quickly. I told the deputy mayor—who at that point was Micho Spring, a good friend of mine—that if the old behaviors continued, I'd be out of there. Micho got the mayor on the line, and when he asked what I needed from him, I replied in very colorful language, "Keep these people the fuck out of my hair." The interference ceased immediately. As a result, I became known as a "white hat"—a good guy who has a reputation for integrity and who gets things done.[4]

As soon as I took over the NDEA, I began to pull the place apart. We laid off between 300 to 400 people who were playing programmatic roles in highly ineffective programs that weren't accomplishing anything. Most importantly, we discovered enormous amounts of unspent HUD money because the programs were so poorly run. Funds had been approved by the mayor and city council, so I secured a ruling from the city's Corporation Counsel that no further approvals were needed for funding that had already been authorized.

All of a sudden, I was sitting there with about $30 million of completely discretionary money. It wasn't difficult to land on a new set of priorities.

## The Way Forward: Community Development Corporations

Community Development Corporations (CDCs) changed the way that most urban development was done—from centralized, government bureaucracies to decentralized neighborhood efforts with private investment.

> Americans have a well-established habit of refreshing their institutions and inventing new forms of cooperation where previous [forms] have been ineffectual. Inner-city housing is the tissue of the neighborhood, a marvelous vehicle for developing the capacity to do things and create relationships.
>
> —*The Christian Science Monitor,*
> "Help and Hope for the Inner City" (1994)

This burgeoning Boston strategy—a beautiful solution for reversing neighborhood decline—fueled the next phase of my work in Boston. The foundation was laid, and the stage was set.

The first CDCs were invented and funded heavily by the Ford Foundation in the 1960s. They saw themselves, and Ford saw them, as comprehensive community institutions that would be concerned about everything in neighborhoods. They were not exclusively housing focused, though housing was a big priority for most. There were only about a dozen or so CDCs by the late 1970s, but they were quite large, such as the prototype Bedford Stuyvesant Restoration Corporation (which Ford's president Frank Thomas led as its first director).

Founded in 1979 by the Ford Foundation and half a dozen partners, LISC was created to test the notion of a privately supported, free-standing, highly skilled intermediary that would provide financial resources and technical assistance to emerging CDCs. It was one of the earliest national intermediaries, followed in 1983 by the Enterprise Foundation and others.

Mike Sviridoff, the founding director of the Local Initiatives Support Corporation (LISC)—about whom I will share more colorful commentary in Chapters 3 and 4—wrote an excellent backgrounder about CDCs in a 1994 piece for *The Public Interest* called "The Seeds of Urban Revival." It stands on its own merit as an excellent definition of one of the major sources of inner-city revitalization in the United States:

The CDC is a non-profit, community-based organization governed by a board consisting primarily of neighborhood residents and business leadership, generally found in distressed neighborhoods, and dedicated to the revitalization of a discrete geographic area usually defined by traditional neighborhood boundaries. [The CDC movement] grew out of a mounting disillusionment in the late sixties with centralized government solutions to local social and economic problems. This new non-profit, community-based corporation would emphasize economic and physical development...as the centerpiece of a broader social design to include housing, health, employment, human services, community rehabilitation, and education.

The birth of the CDC movement in Boston in the early 1980s was beautifully chronicled by Alexander von Hoffman in his 2003 book *House by House, Block by Block: The Rebirth of America's Urban Neighborhoods*:

In Boston, a city that lacked the financial might of New York City, people in nonprofit community groups, business, and government discovered the power of collaborating with one another. Through a series of audacious experiments, unlikely alliances of Bostonians established community development systems in Boston by the early 1980s, before most other cities.

In 1964, the United South End Settlements obtained a grant from the federal government and founded South End Community Development, one of the first community development organizations in the country, to rehabilitate deteriorated row houses for low-income families...In 1970 it was renamed Greater Boston Community Development, Inc. (GBCD was renamed the Community Builders in 1988 and is today a national organization.)

Mel King, prominent among African American leaders who started dozens of CDCs, was an activist leader in Boston during this period. He was elected to the Massachusetts state legislature (1973–82) where he sponsored the authorizing legislation to create two state agencies that provided resources to CDCs. As a result, Massachusetts became unusually hospitable to community development.

At the NDEA, we ramped up support for CDCs and nonprofit housing organizations. We were able to change course very quickly. We couldn't do any worse than the city had been doing with its neighborhood programs. We got such great appreciation from grassroots organizations that had felt largely ignored. There was so much energy pent up among these groups who were thrilled with the city's shift in funding and partnership. This transition was the next chapter in Boston's neighborhood development evolution that made Boston one of the leading cities for grassroots community revitalization and affordable housing in the country.

As I started to do outreach and try to build the kinds of partnerships that we would need to be successful, I encountered this barrier: foundations believed that there was no role for them in housing. The world of community development was not a philanthropic priority for any local foundations. There was a strong commitment at the Ford Foundation, but that was about the extent of national-level interest.

We basically waged an educational campaign to explain and illuminate the tremendous opportunities for philanthropic investment in housing and community development, including by the Boston Foundation. Foundations could provide significant leverage to unleash public and private capital. And, of course, that's exactly what came to pass to a dramatic degree. There are so many foundations now that are participating in one way or another in the development space. We really changed that thinking around by demonstrating with data the impact of these investments.

In part because of our department's effective use of this massive bucket of unspent funds, Marvin Siflinger and his team at HUD saw that we were committed professional leaders. With their confidence restored in both our staff team and the mayor, HUD shifted out of regulatory mode and became our development partners, supporting our efforts wherever possible. Given the city's long history of broken promises and disappointments, we were grateful that HUD was willing to take a chance and give it one more shot. The relationship has been solid ever since.

## An Unlikely Transition:
## From Kevin White to Ray Flynn Administrations (1984)

Kevin White was seriously considering a fifth term of office. I remember so clearly asking him what he wanted to achieve in a fifth term that had not already been accomplished. I don't think he necessarily appreciated my question, but exhausted after four tumultuous terms, Kevin decided not to run.

Ray Flynn's ascension to the mayor's office was both unlikely and enormously significant for the life of the city. Flynn began his political career in City Council representing South Boston. But as he decided to run for higher political office, he needed to commit to building a broader constituency. This also meant that he would have to broaden his views.

Flynn's decision to build a broad, diverse coalition of supporters ended up having huge positive consequences for the city. Political ambitions can overcome big obstacles—for instance, Boston's traditional tribalism. Flynn won the mayoral election thanks to the broad coalition he assembled, and then governed from the same position. The legitimacy he accrued allowed him to overcome difficult and controversial issues and accomplish major initiatives such as the desegregation of public housing with none of the violence that accompanied the desegregation of public schools in the 1970s. My observation is that Ray Flynn may be the most important public figure to improve Boston's racial climate and heal wounds from school desegregation.

I was the only top staff person from the White Administration asked to stay on when Ray Flynn began his first term as mayor in 1984. Many people asked him why he chose me, and his response was, "I've got Grogan, and

> " Grogan...who was often called one of the city's most versatile public officials... [served] as a trouble-shooter for [Mayor Ray] Flynn...and being somewhat of a balancing force...for neighborhood development. He was a holdover from the administration of former mayor, Kevin White.
>
> —*Boston Globe*, "Hub neighborhoods ask: After Grogan, what?" (1985)

he's the whole Harvard Kennedy School of Government all by himself." (Of course, Mayor Flynn was kidding.) I used to say that my full name was "Kevin White holdover Grogan." More to the point, though, Ray Flynn's campaign platform centered on the need for more neighborhood development and employment opportunities for Boston residents. The news media widely captured the sentiment, "If it ain't broke, don't fix it." I had restored credibility to the NDEA, and Mayor Flynn was intent upon keeping it that way.

Mayor Flynn's decision to ask me to stay was huge. Sometimes I still can't believe it. That did so much for me, and it was so unexpected. To this day, it is one of the lucky events that really made a difference in terms of the opportunities I had. I am forever grateful.

Mayor Flynn was wrongly perceived as anti-business because the coalition he put together to get elected included youthful liberals dubbed "sandanistas" by the press. I was honored that he asked me to be his point person with the business community to help him with those relationships. I was dispatched to reach out to business leaders, to keep them engaged, and hopefully to make them feel connected to the city. Business leaders were quite surprised that someone was calling on them from the Flynn administration just wanting to let them know what was going on in the city.

Years later, I asked Mayor Flynn why he had kept me on in his administration to run the NDEA. His answer hinged on the quality of the people I had hired to work in the Boston Community Schools. He thought they were exceptional, the backbone of the city. They were good public servants, and they cared

(Center) City Councillor Charles Yancy, Mayor Ray Flynn, and NDEA Director Paul Grogan with members of a Dorchester neighborhood tenants' council for low-income housing; 1984.

about people. I will forever savor the compliment Mayor Flynn gave me, saying that my leadership of Community Schools—solving problems and taking the program to the next level—was one of the finest acts of public administration he'd ever seen. He called it a "high wire act with no script and no net."

## Closing Thoughts on the City of Boston: Igniting my Passion for Community Development

Inspired new solutions to intractable problems is a wonderfully American phenomenon.

Federal budget cuts made during the Carter and Reagan Administrations—roughly 1977 through 1985—threatened to further decimate urban neighborhoods already struggling to recover from decades of disinvestment and decline. The Community Reinvestment Act, established in 1977, was meant to substitute private capital for federal grants, to provide access to credit in low- and moderate-income neighborhoods. There was just one small problem: there were very few investible organizations or projects or credit-worthy individuals by private sector standards, so banks were not willing to make risky loans.

The nascent CDC movement, which got its start in the late 1960s thanks to the Ford Foundation, was poised to step in to rescue the situation. Small, independent neighborhood-based organizations, typically founded by charismatic leaders, had big ideas but no capital and limited capacity to take on significant projects. But something was just waiting to happen.

When I took over Boston's Neighborhood Development and Employment Agency, I saw this glimmer of hope begin to brighten in communities. When we discovered a significant windfall of unspent block grant funds, and convinced Mayor Kevin White to shift the use of that funding to support CDCs, we helped to ignite and strengthen the CDC movement in Boston.

This defining moment in the early 1980s was the beginning of my lifelong passion for supporting the phenomenal work of community development corporations with capital and capacity. It set the stage for the next step in my career pathway, to lead an intermediary called LISC whose mission was to provide capital and build CDC capacity at a grand scale. Call it lucky timing, but I was well prepared for this next big step by my Boston experience.

My ten years serving in city government demonstrated to me that with determined, creative, and collaborative leadership, a city can be turned back from the brink. It was exhilarating to be a small part of it, and to help develop the careers of dedicated staff working for Community Schools and the NDEA who went on to significant leadership roles in the city. Unlike the one-year federal immersion programs such as the Peace Corps and VISTA, the CDC movement was emerging as a sustainable ecosystem.

I recognize that today many young people are cynical about government and political leaders. I encourage you to park that cynicism on the shelf for one, or two, or ten years, and either enter a public service career or participate in civic life as a volunteer. My city experience opened doors for me that I never could have imagined possible, as you will see for yourself.

# — 3 —

# Taking Community Development to Scale

LOCAL INITIATIVES SUPPORT CORPORATION (LISC)
1986–1998

After a decade working at Boston City Hall for the Kevin White and Ray Flynn administrations, by 1985 I was in my mid-thirties and feeling ready for a new venture, restless and ready for a change. Thanks to these two tremendous mayors, I had the privilege of being very involved in engineering the City of Boston's strategy of working more closely with both the business and the nonprofit community. I was gaining a reputation for leadership using this approach, even beyond Boston.

### Always Say Yes Even If You Want To Say No!
### (You Never Know Who's Listening)

When I learned that LISC was looking for a new national president to follow founding director Mike Sviridoff, I decided to put my hat in the ring. I thought I had a good feel for the job from my work with CDCs and Boston LISC. Stanford still awaited my final decision to start business school that Fall. But running Boston's neighborhood programs had given me a taste for leadership and the tremendous satisfaction of making a palpable difference in the community.

I went to see the head of the search firm Isaacson Miller—John Isaacson, who I knew well—thinking I could ask him if he thought it was worth my while to try to get the LISC job. We had a very nice exploratory meeting. He was charming and respectful. But he said, "You're not ready for this show, you're four or five years from it. I don't recommend that you go for it at this point, but I know you're going to have a great future. There will be another opportunity."

I was very disappointed. But as it turned out, my timing was fortuitous. LISC's high-powered search committee could not agree on a CEO candidate. They had some very attractive applicants from around the country, but the committee was deadlocked.

What happened next is one of my most important life lessons. Bill Edgerly and I were set to sponsor a conference for business leaders in Boston about neighborhood development and the role of the private sector. At the time, Bill was the CEO of Boston's State Street Bank, one of our major corporations, and chairman of the Private Industry Council. He was the top business leader involved in community affairs in those days. It was remarkable what he was willing to do, and he got some very big results.

The purpose of the conference was to stir the idea of doing things differently in Boston, engaging new players to the cause of community development. It was our plan for Bill to keynote the conference in an auditorium full of very influential people. To my great dismay, Bill called me a day or two ahead of the conference to say that he was getting battered on Wall Street and had to go deal with the analysts. He wasn't going to be able to come to our conference.

I rocked back in my chair and said, "Oh my God. The whole thing hinges on you. Who's the CEO we can get to take your place? It's going to be very difficult to get somebody at the last minute. The whole theme of this conference is business involvement." Bill's solution was simply that I should give the speech. I argued that it wouldn't deliver the right message for a city official to make the address, but Bill said, definitively, "You're giving the speech."

What made this another turning point in my career—the most powerful fulfillment of our slogan "be prepared to be lucky"—was that Mike Sviridoff came to Boston for the conference and was very interested in what was going on there. We knew each other slightly. I had worked closely with LISC's Boston chapter, so I was already part of this new kind of institution and group of players emerging in cities to do interesting things.

Apparently, I must have done a good job on the speech because I got tremendous feedback from Sviridoff. He was so impressed that when he went back to New York, he called up the head of the LISC search committee and said, "I've got your person for you. His name is Paul Grogan. He's a high city official in Boston, and why aren't you looking at him?"

Based on that report from Sviridoff, I got a call from John Isaacson saying, "Would you still be open to thinking about the LISC job?" I got on a flight to LaGuardia a day or two later to meet in person with the search committee. We had one more meeting a week later. I got the offer, took the job, and my fiancée Karen Sunnarborg and I packed up our house in Dorchester to move to a fourth-floor walk-up in Brooklyn with a terrific view of the bridge and Lady Liberty.

Back in Boston to wrap things up, I met with Mayor Ray Flynn to let him know that I would be leaving to take the LISC job. He said to me, "I'm surprised you're leaving, because if you stayed, you'd probably be the

---

> LISC has become a leading model for public-private development, funneling more than $3 billion into urban and rural development efforts over the past twenty years...[Grogan] has been the group's public face for the past thirteen years and something of a missionary for the cause, traveling around the country, testifying in Congress, and generally trying to whip up enthusiasm for private-sector investment in troubled neighborhoods.
>
> —*US Banker*, "A Redevelopment Pioneer Reflects" (1999)

---

first non-indigenous mayor of Boston." That statement floored me, but I took it as a huge compliment, and off I went to New York City.

And so began more than three decades of speculation in the media, by politicians, and by Bostonians with political aspirations, about my supposed intentions to run for mayor. Was my career pathway to LISC—followed by Harvard and then the Boston Foundation—simply a prelude to running for office in Boston? This line of thinking was pervasive in the media. Thirty-five years after I left the Flynn Administration, during the Chamber of Commerce's Distinguished Bostonian awards program, then-governor Charlie Baker quipped, "Paul, every single year, when we start to think about mayoral campaigns, we see the current mayor and all the candidates slowly looking over their shoulders: is he going to run this time?"

As LISC's second CEO, I was lucky to lead the organization to its next level of success and scale. Was getting the LISC job a twist of fate? Perhaps. If Bill Edgerly had not had a conflict for our conference, who knows how this story would have ended. I use the saying "be prepared to be lucky" in a lot of talks to illustrate that you can't really dictate results, but you can be ready for opportunities when they arise. That was one of the greatest illustrations of being prepared and incredibly lucky in my career. It opened up unbelievable opportunities.

## New Kids on the Block

By the time I joined LISC in early 1986, the fledgling organization had just celebrated its sixth anniversary. Not bad for an initiative—an experiment, really—that was meant to sunset after five years!

Before diving into my own story, I think it's important to lay down an overview of the key elements of LISC's early history and its formative work with CDCs. I stand on the shoulders of some of the greatest leaders of philanthropy and community development, including Franklin A. (Frank) Thomas, former president of the Ford Foundation; Mitchell (Mike) Sviridoff, who was a Ford Foundation vice president as well as LISC's founder and first CEO; the Rev. Calvin Butts, leader of the Abyssinian Development Corporation in Harlem; Genevieve Brooks, founder of the Mid-Bronx Desperados; and many others.

### Creating an Innovative Intermediary: Local Initiatives Support Corporation

LISC was created by the Ford Foundation in 1979 to challenge the conventional wisdom that government programs were the right vehicles to combat urban poverty. To counter this, LISC was envisioned as an intermediary, a nonprofit organization designed to connect public and private resources to people and places where underinvestment had caused physical blight and concentration of poverty.

The value of large, centralized bureaucracies was the main thesis of the 1964 "War on Poverty" launched during the Lyndon B. Johnson administration. Thousands of public housing projects and many well-meaning welfare programs were created, but by the late 1970s, many of these programs had come to be seen as ineffective. Official poverty rates had declined, but inner cities continued to deteriorate.

What was different in the 1980s? LISC was one of the first national intermediaries established to help overcome the inertia of trying to rebuild urban communities one house and one commercial building at a time.

Although the Ford Foundation was the primary source of funding during the early years of LISC, founding CEO Mike Sviridoff had the idea to get support from national corporations such as Aetna Life & Casualty, International Harvester, and Levi Strauss, to fund projects in a few communities that had organized locally to address issues of poverty. Within just a few months, LISC had raised $10 million and made its first round of loans and grants.

For the first six-plus years of the program, the fledgling LISC program replicated a foundation program officer staffing model, using part-time "fly-

Michael Rubinger (third from left) conducting a neighborhood tour. *Courtesy of LISC.*

in-fly-out" personnel as the *modus operandi*. It was a great deal for local communities because national LISC paid for everything. In those early years, local involvement consisted of volunteer advisory committees formed by good citizens in those communities. But they weren't initially expected to help with fundraising at all.

Michael Rubinger was one of LISC's first employees. At the time, LISC was meant to be an experimental extension of the Ford Foundation's community development strategy: seek out individual CDCs and fund their work. That focus sent Michael criss-crossing the country in search of investible CDCs.

As its model of partnering locally with businesses, government, and community organizations—funded 100% by philanthropy—caught on across the country, LISC grew quickly. By 1985, LISC was working with multiple community-based organizations in about thirty cities. But staff were still parachuting in, staying a day or two, and going home. Work stalled without a local shepherd.

Even with this marginally effective approach, however, LISC could show (and count) results, documenting increases in the magnitude of community vitality by working with and through CDCs. Ford could have continued to fund CDCs directly, as it had with some of the first CDCs in New York City. But with funding and the imprimatur of the Ford Foundation, LISC set a new national standard for the use of intermediaries to carry out the important work of financing and supporting CDCs on behalf of charitable foundations.

By focusing on larger projects and collaborating with community groups, LISC changed the paradigm for community development. This new national/local ecosystem supporting a comprehensive approach to community development was key to scaling the work of urban revitalization, and to making it sustainable.

*Building the Capacity of Community Development Corporations*

One of the most important things that drew me to the opportunity to lead LISC was the level of excitement growing nationally in the mid-1980s about the potential for the self-help community development movement. I had seen that innovation take root first-hand in Boston. The Ford Foundation's early investments in CDCs, and its equally important investment in the LISC intermediary designed to support their work, was beginning to show impact well beyond the theory of a new idea. Urban groups started

---

" Mitchell Sviridoff became convinced that CDCs could be a catalyst for the economic and social revival of inner-city neighborhoods. "

—*House by House, Block by Block: The Rebirth of America's Urban Neighborhoods* by Alexander von Hoffman

---

coming forward in a second wave of CDCs after the initial Ford Foundation investments in the 1960s and 1970s started producing visible results.

Incredible resident leaders began to surface to take charge of their own communities, which was very attractive to people against a backdrop of total pessimism about cities and disenchantment with government. It was a shiny new thing building new housing in some of the worst neighborhoods. CDCs were moving beyond project-by-project strategies and rehabbing entire blocks of dilapidated housing.

At first, bankers were resistant to financing CDC projects. They had tried financing CDCs in the sixties and concluded that the approach didn't work. Our rebuttal was that twenty years had gone by, and it was worth giving it another shot. LISC's strategy of putting business leaders in touch with outstanding community leaders ultimately inspired other sources of local financing.

LISC was fortunate to develop the tools that allowed us to become a big player. With LISC's help in the form of loans, grants, and technical assistance, the number of CDCs grew rapidly from just a handful in the mid-1970s to nearly 4,000 by 2000. LISC's relationship with CDCs was supportive, not just aimed at providing financing for housing, but also at increasing the organizational capacity of the CDCs themselves.

Today, there are more than 17,000 urban and rural CDCs in the United States that employ more than 265,000 people and which have assets of more than $17 billion.[4] Many have transformed urban communities from extreme blight into bustling, vital neighborhoods by bringing in shopping centers, educational programs, daycare centers, and senior facilities in addition to affordable housing.

## It's Not a Cliché: What Happens the First Hundred Days Matters

The fact that I was hired without a New York network was quite remarkable to me. It was more than a little daunting.

> Grogan emerged on the scene when the community development movement was nascent, when in fact the United States was having doubts about whether it could deal with its most serious problems, particularly domestic.
>
> —Peter Goldmark, former president of the Rockefeller Foundation

I started getting briefed on every aspect of the organization, talking to people all over the country. The New York office didn't appear to be a place where anything much was happening. As I walked around a mostly empty office for the first time, all I could hear was a single typewriter clacking in the background.

It turned out that we were in a precarious position financially. In fact, there really wasn't enough money to meet payroll. The Ford Foundation was our only source of funding at that point. We had a maximum of three or four months of operating reserves before the organization would have to fold.

What was actually going on in the boiler room was not good. Nobody knew this on the staff or the Board. Even though I wasn't aware of the situation when I accepted the CEO position, I knew I had to act quickly, with focused determination, to make LISC work financially. I believed in the mission, believed in the promise of CDCs, and could rely to an extent on my experiences in Boston pulling troubled organizations back from the brink.

I had a very tough first Board meeting when I presented our financial situation. Some people were angry, and they kind of took it out on me. There was talk about creating a special committee of the Board to look at the finances.

This situation was threatening the viability of the whole organization. After this difficult meeting, Michael Rubinger, who was a key member of the national staff team, suggested that I meet with every Board member individually to reassure them and gain their support. I met with about twenty people, some by telephone, but most Board members were New Yorkers at that

Paul Grogan with Jake Mascotte, chairman of the LISC board, in the New York offices of the Continental Company; 1986.

point. My message was "You brought me down here to lead this organization and you must give me an opportunity to fix this problem. If I don't get it right after whatever period of time you want to set, we'll go in another direction."

LISC Board chairman Jake Mascotte, who was then chairman and CEO of the Continental Corporation, was crucial in this deliberation. He said, "All right, we're going to back off. Let Paul do his thing. Let's be as helpful as we can, and then we'll go on from there."

That ended up working. What made it work was money, of course. The Ford Foundation decided to make a big bet on us. We got an enormous grant. I was visiting Martha's Vineyard when Frank Thomas (then president of Ford) gave me a heads up. While we were swimming together, he said, "By the way, at our board meeting last week, we gave you $5.65 million in grants and $1.5 million in Program Related Investments [PRIs, or loans]." For the moment, and for the foreseeable future, it significantly improved the organization's financial problems.

But the deeper problem was that the whole LISC operation, nationally and locally, was centralized and had been paid for by Ford and the initial tranche of corporate funding raised by Ford. These grants paid the salaries of the national program officers and grants to local offices. It wasn't a sustainable situation.

Then and now, the Ford Foundation sees itself as a place that seeds and invests in ideas, innovations, and institutions. LISC was one of several innovations that Ford helped to create in the late 1970s and early 1980s. Another example is the Grameen Bank in Bangladesh: like LISC, it was formed out of a set of ideas, and then became a behemoth doing many more things than were initially envisioned. In the 1980s, it was a well-established life cycle for Ford to provide seed funding, encourage institutions to find new funding, and then begin to wind down its own support so it could redirect resources to more new ideas. There are hundreds of organizations around the world that can tell a similar story. My friend Darren Walker, Ford's current president, is fond of saying that "this is the arc of the Foundation."

It was very clear that we needed to diversify our funding sources if we were going to move forward and grow. To actually realize the promise of this extraordinary experiment, we had to have financial support from multiple sources.

As I mentioned in the introduction to this chapter describing the design of LISC, our local partners were not required to raise money. In a rather perverse twist, this new private urban poverty program operated like a welfare state. Ford had the money to pay for everything and was willing to do it. We had to make a fairly quick and energetic move. We didn't even have a development director. There hadn't been a need for anybody to raise money.

## A Grand Bargain Inspired by the Big Three: Chicago, Boston, and New York

Mike Sviridoff's management style was high energy and hands off. He would fly around the country, make a deal in a new community, and then tell staff to figure it out. Our national program officers were mostly New Yorkers who shuttled back and forth to whatever city they were working in. Each person had several assignments.

Andy Ditton and Michael Rubinger were key, both to this early "fly-in" strategy and to the transformation that soon followed. For several years, Andy ran Chicago and worked with the western cities. Michael ran Boston and the eastern cluster from New York. Michael was one of the first employees at LISC, and Andy Ditton was a rising star in Chicago.

I decided to take a massive swing through the country with these two senior leaders. It didn't take very long for us to look at the situation and conclude that we couldn't match the organization's vision with this kind of part-time staff structure. It became increasingly clear that the original staffing model wasn't working. It was too shallow, severely lacking in scale and impact. Many of the local organizations LISC funded were not even CDCs—they were small nonprofits with an interest in community development—and did not have the capacity to produce housing or other revitalization programs. There was confusion among local volunteer advisory councils about national vs. local roles, and about funding. Our conclusion was that LISC couldn't be successful over the long term with the existing structure.

Taking a comprehensive approach to community development, collaborating with city government, getting to know a range of local financial institutions, and getting foundations to the table—essentially forming relationships with a whole new set of actors—exemplified what Chicago, Boston, and New York were already doing at scale in the 1980s. In many ways, these cities set the standard and served as prototypes for restructuring LISC to become a sustainable institution capable of greater impact.

One of LISC's first and most important early partnerships was with Chicago (1984). Andy Ditton was working for Neighborhood Housing Services running one of the organization's three Chicago offices. Andy had begun looking at ways to attract corporate dollars into affordable housing projects to reduce reliance on philanthropy. As Andy tells this part of the Chicago office's story-of-origin, he hadn't even heard of LISC when Mike Sviridoff called to ask him for a meeting. Part of the reason for Chicago's "hidden LISC" was that the national office was still using part-time stringers to staff local programs. Sviridoff was keen to open a full-time local office there.

The Chicago LISC office got started with a $2.5 million grant that Andy secured from the John D. and Catherine T. MacArthur Foundation, soon followed by millions from other philanthropic sources. Within a year, Andy had figured out how to move forward on a corporate engagement strategy. His solution was the Chicago Equity Fund which relied on a federal regulation that accelerated depreciation for certain kinds of real estate, including affordable housing, to attract corporate investment.

In addition to corporate support, Chicago LISC had the support of the city and the young, ambitious Mayor Richard M. Daley. Mayor Daley had come into power by building a coalition that included influential progressives like local PR maven Marilyn Katz who had the mayor's ear and convinced him to support LISC's approach to community-based development.

By the early 1990's, the Chicago LISC office had gained a reputation for creativity and results. The program was attracting a lot of attention and talent, including a young community organizer named Barack Obama who LISC tried to recruit. Nearly two decades later, I had a chance encounter with then-President Obama who, to my astonishment, recognized me and

(Center) Vice President Al Gore, Paul Grogan, and Chicago Mayor Richard Daley, with (far right) U. S. Representative Dick Durbin (D-IL), visiting Chicago's South Side in 1993.

asked if I remembered when I interviewed him for the LISC Chicago job. Of course I did! He didn't take the job, but I told him this: "The evidence shows that you did the right thing!"

Another important early partnership was with Boston. I was still working for the City of Boston in 1985 when LISC opened a program office there. Michael Rubinger headed up the Boston program from New York. Then Carol Glazer came on the scene. She graduated from the Harvard Kennedy School of Government in 1985, aware of LISC and what it was trying to accomplish. She boldly approached the head of the local advisory committee and pitched running the Boston program. Boston Edison hired Carol as an intern and agreed to pay her salary as the local LISC program director.

Shortly after I started at LISC in 1986, I put Boston on my national tour list and met with Carol to hear about her vision for the Boston program.

It was strong, based on the perspective that each site needed to have local staff to be successful. As I continued my national tour and came to the same conviction, it seemed that we had already secured talent in Boston and demonstrated an early proof point for how much better a decentralized model could work. Carol remained a loaned executive in Boston for four years until I recruited her to the national team in New York.

Our work in New York City might be the most striking of all. Just as I was transitioning to New York, people like Kathy Wylde (Partnership for New York) and Mark Willis (NYC Department of Housing Preservation and Development) were eager to get LISC more involved in New York City. Mayor Ed Koch called for a major new housing program, so Mark Willis and I scoped it out on the back of a napkin. I was prepared for this conversation. My experience in Boston while leading the Neighborhood Development & Employment Agency—working with CDCs to "batch" properties rather than address properties one at a time—dramatically accelerated the redevelopment process. The City of New York agreed to batch properties and provide project financing, which revolutionized the pace at which abandoned buildings and entire neighborhoods could be saved. With the luck of timing, we just happened to have the perfect solution that New York City was looking for.

The first big move I made as the new president of LISC was to put in front of the Board a very different concept that had a lot of inherent risks and implications, especially financial. I essentially made the argument that we can either do a few more good things under the current structure, or we could create a new structure designed to grow the scale of the program and develop some intensity around neighborhood development and housing in urban communities.

We also concluded that LISC should move away from the original comprehensive concept of community development and focus on housing because it was a huge priority for urban neighborhoods in the 1980s. We had found that improving housing markets made all sorts of things possible that wouldn't otherwise have been considered. Housing isn't everything, but it's very powerful: negative if housing is declining, positive if you can turn it around.

We proceeded to develop a new brand, which I called "a new grand bargain." We needed to take a fresh look at a way to have far more impact, to be more consequential. As strategic planning processes go, this ended up being a very good one. Taking our cues from Boston, Chicago, and New York, the focus shifted from a project-by-project approach to entire neighborhoods and communities. We formed a consensus around the need to utterly restructure the finances of the program and find a way to bring higher expectations and greater results to the work. We needed to shift from a centralized to a decentralized organizational structure. Last (but not least), if we wanted to make a difference across the nation, it was a necessary step to challenge our cluster of thirty communities to take this more seriously.

I went back out around the country a second time to meet with local advisory boards. We had a "come to Jesus" moment with all of them. We didn't invite a lot of input from anybody, we just laid out the plan. We basically said, "It's up or out." The current model is not effective. You need to take LISC seriously, put much more attention and resources into it, have a local staff presence, pay for the program with at least 50% local dollars, and set expectations at a very different pace. This is our offer. We said at the outset, "You may not be up for this. There won't be any hard feelings if you aren't. This is the new game plan; you can be part of it, or you can say no thanks."

At a dinner in Pittsburgh hosted by the city's local advisory committee, one guest said what most people were probably thinking: "This all sounds terrific, but how are you going to get this done without Mike Sviridoff?" I took that speculation in stride. I said, "Well, let's see."

We shuttered about half the groups. There weren't hard feelings, as I recall. It was just a recognition on the part of some communities that they weren't ready for this level of time and investment, or that community development wasn't their philanthropic priority.

## Institution Building: Restructuring LISC

Our new direction was anchored by the hybrid approach of local offices supported by central leadership. The model was central to the new strategy. We struck the right balance, taking advantage of the growing passion of local residents to strengthen their communities and pairing it with the growing capacity of the national organization. We created a pathway to sustainability by getting multiple institutions invested in the fate of a community, and in the CDCs themselves.

In the early stage, LISC had great expectations and a lot of money but not great results. By cutting the number of program sites back to the critical few places we thought had real potential, we made allies and partners for our important community development work. We recognized that our new approach wasn't going to work for everybody, and that we would dilute the program if we included programs that weren't really committed to what we were trying to accomplish.

We got exactly what we wanted: about a dozen serious programs, locally staffed, willing to share the fundraising burden. By insisting on local staff and local leadership, we created strong ecosystems of support. It was under-

At the beginning, Mike Sviridoff cast a wide net across the country to identify communities that could potentially step up their development work with Ford Foundation funding through LISC. When Grogan took over in 1986, it was definitely time to take a more strategic approach, both nationally and locally, by hiring local staff and pruning the number of local programs to focus on a smaller group of CDCs ready, willing, and able to scale their development efforts.

—Ellen Gilligan, former LISC staff and president & CEO
of The Greater Milwaukee Foundation

stood that long-term impact would require hiring high quality local staff, eventually more than one in each program. We hired exceptional people, some of whom were already working at community development organizations in those sites and others who were imported, to create a cadre of local program executive directors living and working on location.

The structural decisions we made across the organization as part of "a new grand bargain" turned out (in hindsight) to have been pivotal to what LISC was then able to achieve in the next decade. Reducing the number of sites led to tremendous future growth. It also inspired greater awareness among funders that housing and community development priorities did not fall exclusively within the domain of government.

Andy Ditton, Michael Rubinger, and I had the mindset that we wanted to grow the organization significantly. We didn't want to run a static program for a little while only to close it down for lack of performance or money.

Any decentralized organization has options or choices about how to put things together structurally depending on what they're trying to accomplish. We could have spun these programs off locally as independent entities. Some people were in favor of going in that direction. What we decided was that LISC programs would remain part of a single organization. Uneven local quality and the absence of a track record in borrowing were among the reasons for creating the structure of a single LISC corporation. We wanted to have more direction over what was happening programmatically, and we recognized that national LISC could not, in good conscience, take on a lot of debt on behalf of these nascent programs if they were not directly accountable.

The national organization's support took many forms. We did a lot to develop talent across the country, including convening people, developing research papers, and introducing staff to best practices in community development. We got national technical assistance programs going quickly, and they immediately paid off. LISC production began to scale up during my first year as president.

As LISC's lending and grantmaking activities began to mushroom, we needed someone who could handle the growing complexity of the financial operation. That's when I hired Ed Lloyd to be LISC's first CFO and the first African American senior staff officer.

The stupendous growth of the organization after that point, in parallel to the stupendous growth of the CDC movement, is at least in part due to our decision to challenge people to either make a larger commitment or just say goodbye. We nailed that one. LISC became a very different place to work. It became *the* place to work if you were a community development professional.

## Creating the Strategic Triangle: Communications, Public Policy & Fundraising (Powered by Data)

At the same time that I was working on restructuring the staffing of the LISC organization, I also needed to figure out how to elevate and amplify the work of community development corporations in their own communities across the country. I was keen to help transform the nascent community development movement into a replicable social change tool. I had the beginnings of a blueprint in my mind that would include a national communications program and fundraising campaign that could fuel national public policy work.

One of my first hires at the national office was Patty Foley as Senior Vice President for External Affairs. A mutual friend thought Patty's background in policy and fundraising, and her work as a liaison between Senator John Kerry and Massachusetts mayors, would be a perfect fit with my plan to create a department of external relations. He was right.

Mayors and governors were big fans of LISC. We were bringing financial resources to their cities and states through both low-interest loans and grants, which took some of the pressure off municipal and state budgets. That, plus the time I spent cultivating relationships with these political leaders, paved the way for LISC to develop campaign strategies targeting federal policy. Advo-

> Paul understood that public policy had to be an important part of our activities—influencing legislation, regulations, developing programs, directing resources. And people have to know what you do, to understand that you're having an impact. Communications was a big part of that. It was a revelation for LISC.
>
> —Michael Rubinger, former LISC president & CEO (retired)

cacy and communications were two very important tools necessary to effect change; our approach resonated with politicians and policymakers.

I also had the great good fortune to hire Benson "Buzz" Roberts, a whiz kid on housing policy. Buzz gave LISC a vigorous policy presence on Capitol Hill.

Our fundraising program, which we called the Campaign for Communities, got started in the early 1990s under the leadership of Susan Shapiro who became our Vice President of Development. Our goal was to raise a jaw-dropping $200 million. We had every reason to believe that it was possible in a strong economy. Our communities needed it, and we could make the case.

Prior to launch, the groundwork included working with national media to follow LISC's program work in New York City and some other major markets like Chicago and Kansas City. We also hosted press events in Washington D.C., inviting mayors and governors to meet with people like Speaker of the House Dan Rostenkowski and Senate Majority Leader George Mitchell. It was crucial to the public phase of our fundraising campaign that policy makers, the corporate community, and others had a good sense about what community development was accomplishing and the leadership role that LISC was playing to help rebuild America's neighborhoods.

The Campaign for Communities closed out having raised $297 million in just over three years, more than a year ahead of schedule.

It was a speech Paul made at one of the last two high schools standing in Gary, Indiana. The premise of the gathering was that we were considering a Gary LISC program.

The auditorium was packed, one hundred percent local Black folks except for the two of us. Paul started speaking about what community development meant and what local empowerment could produce. He got into one of these rolling speeches that I had seen him make a few times before. It was unbelievable. He was using the "call and response" approach in his speech, going at the audience and asking them to respond, which they did in a mass outpouring to whatever Paul was saying.

I don't recall the specifics of what he said to the audience. It was nearly forty years ago! All I recall is this White guy up front sounding like a gospel preacher, just blasting out a message. The audience got so energized and so into it. It was one of the best speeches I've ever seen anybody give.

You could roll up every one of his leadership talents into one thing: *the ability to inspire people.* It separated Paul from the pack. It was remarkable how good Paul was at communicating facts, communicating the need, communicating the solution, and wrapping it all up in an energized, inspirational delivery.

From my perspective, this is the immense value that Paul brought to the community development industry and to what happened afterward at the Boston Foundation. It was a community game changer—for politicians, for mass audiences, and for corporate titans in city after city.

—Andy Ditton, former LISC executive and retired Citi managing director

Paul Grogan keynoting the annual meeting of the Urban League of Eastern Massachusetts (Roxbury).

# — 4 —

# Tools in the Community Development Toolkit

Embarking on a fast-paced transformation of LISC's ambition to achieve national scale would require some bold moves. We were lucky, and well prepared, to push for passage of federal legislation that would fundamentally change the way that affordable housing was financed in the United States. We took a significant and bold move to take a chance on creating an entire organization to implement the new program. It worked! And then, within the next decade, we were poised and prepared to take

> In the characteristics of transformational change, I usually focus on tenacity, because I think that's the hardest one. Leading a transition assumes there is heat that comes with it. If you're making a change that matters, you're going to make some people angry. Managing organizational (reputation, financial) and personal risk is an essential element of leading transformation. Said another way, you have to be willing to figure out how to make a transition and be able to communicate what you're doing so that others can join the transformation.
>
> —Alberto Ibargüen, president, The Knight Foundation

first-mover advantage when new funding and financing opportunities became available to support the community development work on the ground led by our local programs. These major initiatives are described in some detail in this part of my story.

## Federal Public Policy Win: Low Income Housing Tax Credit (1986) and the National Equity Fund (1987)

In the late 1960s and early 1970s, the Johnson administration's War on Poverty was funded almost entirely by the federal government. By the late 1970s, and into the 1980s, large national foundations—particularly the Ford Foundation—joined the cause, believing that government solutions had been to that point largely ineffective.

Based on my experiences working for the City of Boston, I had learned an abiding and powerful lesson: the best way to get solid results on virtually any issue was through partnerships among government, nonprofit organizations, and businesses. I came to understand clearly that you had to deal with government to be successful in the community development world, or really in any arena having to do with anti-poverty work in the nonprofit sector.

The most important piece of federal legislation passed during my thirteen-year tenure at LISC was the Low Income Housing Tax Credit (LIHTC). Our LISC team was instrumental in getting the original legislation passed by Congress in 1986, and six years later helping to secure it as a permanent source of financing for low-income housing. LIHTC also spawned LISC's most successful affiliate, the National Equity Fund (NEF).

I would like to tell you both stories, of LIHTC and NEF, as a significant demonstration of what can happen as the result of the public and private sectors working together, the ambition of a talented team of staff, and the courageous leadership of a nonprofit board.

*Low Income Housing Tax Credit*

It was enormously significant to the community development field to get the Low-Income Housing Tax Credit (LIHTC) passed. It was highly implausible that it would fly. But getting the legislation passed, and creating a novel implementation strategy, showed what can happen when nonprofit organizations are willing to take risks and explore new avenues when there aren't good alternatives. That's what happened here. Thanks to Patty Foley, we were prepared with research and a communications plan that explained the need and potential impact.

A group of people, which included LISC, the Enterprise Foundation, and state housing finance agencies, decided to test the possibility of attaching legislation to a significant tax bill that Congress was considering in 1986. Because of the success of the Chicago program, LISC had an important ally in Congressman Dan Rostenkowski, who happened to be chairing the House Ways and Means Committee. Rostenkowski had already seen first-hand the potential of an equity fund to attract meaningful corporate investment. Although the 1986 Tax Reform Act wiped out most of the federal funding for multi-family housing, the housing tax credit made the cut, almost as a footnote. It created a significant boost for CDCs and other

The Low Income Housing Tax Credit (LIHTC) program is perhaps the most important federal resource for developing and rehabilitating affordable housing in the United States today. Originally enacted as part of the Tax Reform Act of 1986, legislated to sunset after three years, it was renewed several times and ultimately made permanent in 1993. Even now—some thirty years later—LIHTC enjoys tremendous bipartisan support. LIHTC finances about 90% of all new affordable housing development.

> ...[S]ome experts think that the way to restore American urban neighborhoods is to expand the Low Income [Housing] Tax Credit and provide grants for technical assistance to the local groups that would best deploy the resulting investments. Block by block, cities could become places people want to live in once more.
>
> —*Business Week*, "Bringing Hope Back to the 'Hood'" (1996)

nonprofits to develop affordable rental housing, which was (and is) a perennial crisis in this country.

The Tax Reform Act of 1986 was signed into law on October 22, 1986. While the focus on affordable housing was key, equally important was access to new sources of capital and the ability to use the tax credit to spur broader neighborhood revitalization. For LISC, it was a huge organizational lift as well as a new financing vehicle.

At first, the private sector wasn't interested in taking advantage of the housing credit. It was brand new, and nobody really knew how it was going to operate. Congress gave it a three-year life span, essentially requiring a sunset, which was a huge negative factor. When private sector people looked at the risk involved, their assessment was that projects would default if the tax credit wasn't extended beyond three years.

Because there wasn't another major tax bill before Congress in 1989, it was even harder than the first time to get the extension. LISC's decentralized network across the country was an incredible advantage. Both staff and local advisory board members mobilized in some key localities to apply real political pressure to get the extension passed. The biggest example of us flexing our local muscle was our relationship with Mayor Richard Daley. Chicago had always been an all-star program.

One of the great ironies of this story is that the three-year limit ended up being a huge benefit for us and for the Enterprise Foundation, another intermediary founded in 1982 by Maryland developer Jim Rouse. Because

(Left to right) Massachusetts Congressman Patrick Kennedy, Massachusetts Senator John Kerry, Communities in Schools founder Bill Milliken, Paul Grogan, and Habitat for Humanity founder Millard Fuller with President Bill Clinton in the oval office signing a housing bill, 1993.

there was no competition from the private sector, it was not hard to get the credits that were distributed by state housing finance agencies. Few came to the party, so out of necessity we had the field to ourselves. We got a big head start in the business of syndicating tax credits.

When a real market formed, as it did in 1993 when the credits were made permanent under President Clinton, the whole landscape changed drastically.

We were thrilled about the president's decision, but we went from having no competition to having a private market form very quickly. I'd have to say, from today's vantage point, we met that competition very successfully. We developed the capacity and an appeal that worked quite well. In addition to providing money for housing, and providing capital for LISC to do larger projects, this ended up being a major source of revenue for LISC operations and program support.

Paul Grogan (left) with President and Mrs. Clinton (center) at the ribbon cutting for the Mahlon Martin Community Apartments, built in 1923 and renovated in 1995 using LIHTCs by LISC in partnership with the Downtown Little Rock CDC.

## National Equity Fund

By the time I joined LISC in 1986, Andy Ditton had already been working on getting the LIHTC passed and had a prescient head start on the build-out of a national equity fund based on his experience launching the Chicago Equity Fund. I made Andy Ditton an officer on the national staff as the LIHTC program was getting off the ground. His biggest responsibility was to get this tax credit to work, which we did together.

Because the private sector wasn't interested in the product, we decided to test whether the new program worked. The numbers were in our favor as we weighed the decision to proceed. It was clear we'd have to do it ourselves—a crucial decision point because we had not anticipated filling a private sector vacuum. But we couldn't let our success in getting the legislation passed falter for lack of a distribution system. We decided after much agonizing

The National Equity Fund (NEF) was created in 1987 as an affiliate of LISC to syndicate the Low Income Housing Tax Credit. Its mission is to create and deliver innovative, collaborative financial solutions to expand the creation and preservation of affordable housing. While its core business is as a lender and equity investor in primarily multi-family affordable housing, NEF also offers a range of financial solutions to help close the low- and middle-income affordable housing gap.

to go into the business ourselves, to form a subsidiary company that would syndicate the tax credits that got awarded to both nonprofit and for-profit developers, and then sell those credits in the private secondary market.

The LISC board was meeting in Florida in early December 1986. Andy was ready. Sort of. The pitch was persuasive, the presentation smooth, except for the fact that Andy had left his posters—old-school presentation style nearly forty years ago—in a taxi.

Between the two of us, we walked through the presentation with no props and secured the Board's approval to proceed with creating the simply named National Equity Fund (NEF).

We created the first LIHTC fund within NEF in January 1987 before anyone else really understood what this new approach was all about. The first task was to put together a limited partnership of corporate investors that would agree to purchase a certain number of credits to get this thing off the ground. It wasn't easy to get the first fund going. There was a lot of skepticism in the business community. Often we heard, "We know this is really a grant, but we're letting you guys pretend it's an investment."

We were prepared to be lucky. LISC's Board chair Jake Mascotte led a recruitment campaign to find a group of companies that would participate in a pilot for low-income housing. Jake cashed in every chip he had with fellow corporate CEOs to get this to happen. He put his own company's resources to work even though the Continental Corporation would not benefit from the tax credit. He was our hero in helping that first corporate fund come together. It was an extraordinary personal and corporate commitment on Jake's part. With great effort, we secured a pool of tax credit equity of about $13 million from five or six companies that agreed to participate. We launched the program with that as our initial tax credit partnership.

NEF closed its first LIHTC deal in Kansas City, Missouri, on September 30, 1987.

By October 1987, we were ready to publicly unveil our first NEF fund—also the first fund in the nation—to a broader audience of investors and projects. We were prepared, but not so lucky in our timing. October 19, 1987, came to be known as "Black Monday" when the stock market crashed. We were in the middle of a press conference with about two dozen reporters when suddenly a room full of pagers started beeping (no cell phones then!). One by one, the reporters split out of the room to call in to their respective media. And then they just took off. We can laugh about it now, but that was a really devastating situation for a little organization that put out a big idea.

There was skepticism for some time in the corporate community, but we proved them wrong when the investment returns started to flow. LIHTC proved to be an enormous public policy success with transforming effects on housing, and on the nonprofit development organizations. Coupled with that, the private sector realized that LISC was essential to the process. This was one case where the nonprofits had a lot of influence: the tax credit program wasn't going to happen without nonprofit leadership.

The business leaders who served on the NEF Board were deeply involved in fundraising, including then-chairman David Stanley who was the CEO of Payless Cashways. David had gotten acquainted with Warren Buffett, so he called Buffett for a meeting to interest him in this new low-income housing tax credit.

Buffett didn't know anything about LIHTC. He'd never heard of it. He was kind of intrigued, though, and the result was an initial $25 million investment. This never would have happened without Buffet believing that

> When LISC decided to create the National Equity Fund, Paul asked me to chair it and to help raise money from corporations. We set stretch goals that were quite a reach because companies thought the program was charity. That all changed when we convinced Warren Buffett to become an investor. He cemented our legitimacy. It's very clear that this is a "but for" situation: it wouldn't have happened without us. We directly caused the creation of thousands of homes for needy Americans.
>
> —David Stanley, former chair of the National Equity Fund

the NEF strategy could be profitable. Buffett's credibility was a huge boost. To operate at this level with these institutions and these kinds of people took the community development housing world to a different place. Several years later, Buffett decided to invest $300 million in NEF, establishing widespread credibility for the equity fund's success as a good investment in affordable housing.

One amusing note. When we went to Omaha to meet with Buffett, his HQ demonstrated his reputation for understated humility. His office had all the charm of a small-town dentist's office. There was nothing about it that would have said, "Boy, this guy's on top of his game." He was completely receptive and charming. This was such a great example of humility.

As the Omaha visit was breaking up, people were focusing on transportation to get to the airport. I'm sitting right next to Buffett and he says, "Paul, come with me. I'll call you a cab." So he starts leafing through the Yellow Pages, finds the phone number, dials up the taxi company on his rotary phone, and the cab arrives to whisk us back to the airport.

Here's another piece of the Buffett story that was extraordinary. David Stanley appealed to Buffett to spend a day with us in Washington. David explained the precariousness of the LIHTC and asked him to come to Washington with us and meet with key legislators. Remarkably, Buffett agreed to do it.

(Left to right) Housing Secretary Jack Kemp, NEF Director Doug Guthrie, Paul Grogan, President George H.W. Bush, Warren Buffett, and NEF Board Chair David Stanley at the White House; 1992.

We hired a car to drive us around the city. We met with George H. W. Bush who was president at the time. He met with us completely owing to Buffett's cachet. It registered with the Bush team that tax credits were important and effective tools.

Just as I was nearing the end of my years at LISC in 2000, NEF was searching for a new president. Joe Hagan was well prepared and got the job. He had worked at the Ohio Housing Finance Agency just as the LIHTCs were created and was responsible for allocating the credits. He co-founded the Ohio Capital Corporation to attract corporate investment into Ohio and had run Bank One Community Development Corporation. I authorized his hiring right before I left for Boston and Harvard.

The rest is an amazing story of investment and production of affordable housing, as well as upstreaming support for parent LISC. Part of NEF's success was hiring people who had a skillset in the business of syndication. Today, Chicago-based NEF has syndicated more than 3,000 deals and invested nearly $23 billion, which in turn has produced more than 230,000 units of affordable housing in the continental U.S. plus Puerto Rico, Washington D. C., and the U.S. Virgin Islands. Since inception, NEF has upstreamed more than $225 million in grants to support LISC's nationwide community development work.

Was it luck? Perhaps a small dose at the beginning. We jumped into the tax credits and created NEF without any assurance that it would work, or that the tax credits would be anything more than a small three-year federal program. All that worked out just fine with our advocacy in Washington. But

Paul Grogan and President Bill Clinton in Little Rock.

the key decision way back in 1987 was attaching NEF to LISC as an affiliate, creating an engine for the community development sector and a pipeline of unrestricted resources to deploy across all LISC programs.

The success of NEF illustrates the special quality of LISC, the capacities and credibility it developed. All over the country, we were able to exercise that kind of clout, and to do it in a classy mission-oriented way.

## Diversifying Financing and Funding Tools: LIMAC/Community Development Trust and the National Community Development Initiative

The Low Income Housing Tax Credit and National Equity Fund proved to be big leaps in a new direction toward LISC's long-term sustainability. Here you can see LISC starting to use multiple financing mechanisms traditionally used by the private sector, adapted by LISC, to meet the capital needs of the nonprofit development sector.

But there was more work to do to fulfill the Ford Foundation's mandate—and our imperative for growth—to diversify LISC's funding sources. Three major initiatives led the way.

When Ed Lloyd was CFO at LISC, the organization created fundraising "rounds" to establish steady and consistent cash flow over the course of a year. According to Ed, "We always had cash flow. This to me was innovative. Not all organizations are financially sophisticated enough to understand this approach, but the model provided stable resources for our core operations."

About the same time that LIHTC was passed into law and we created our National Equity Fund affiliate, we decided that we also needed a debt instrument to facilitate financing of local projects. That led to the creation of the Local Initiatives Managed Assets Company (LIMAC) with a $1.5 million low-interest loan from the Ford Foundation. LIMAC offers another illustration of how LISC knitted need and opportunity together, and also demonstrated a different organizational strategy: a spin-off today known as the Community Development Trust.

Several years later, the National Community Development Initiative (NCDI) was perhaps the biggest boost to expand and diversify funding for LISC operations and local community development work. This venture was the brainchild of Peter Goldmark, then president of the Rockefeller Foundation.

### Local Initiatives Managed Assets Company (LIMAC) and Community Development Trust (CDT)

LISC was among the first nonprofit organizations to utilize Program Related Investments (PRIs), "foundation speak" for a loan from a charitable endowment. At first, very few foundations were willing to experiment with PRIs. (Once again, the Ford Foundation was a leader in using this creative debt instrument.)

As PRIs began to drive a lot of demand for projects, our borrowing capacity increased. We got a major boost from the Boston-based Hyams Foundation whose executive director at the time, Beth Smith, saw the wisdom of recycling philanthropic dollars. At one point, LISC was one of the largest PRI borrowers in America.

Using low-interest PRIs to write down the cost of affordable housing projects was one of the big ideas when the Local Initiatives Managed Assets Company (LIMAC) was established as a LISC affiliate in 1986. LIMAC was created under the leadership of Michael Rubinger to purchase, repackage, and sell loans from local community development groups. Eventually LIMAC began to securitize the loans as well, investing its own capital for credit enhancement.

It was slow going at first for LIMAC until 1995 when we had the good sense to hire the brilliant Judd Levy as president. Judd had by that time already had an interesting career. After graduating from Harvard Business School, he ran Merrill Lynch's national public finance division. He retired early to buy and run an inn in Vermont with his wife, Susan. We lured Judd away from this bucolic life to run LIMAC when he was in his late fifties, proving it is never too late to embark on a career in community service.

Judd took LIMAC to the next level of scale. As investment opportunities grew, Judd recommended creating a for-profit REIT (Real Estate Investment Trust) focused on community development. I supported his somewhat risky but innovative idea—the first REIT in the community development industry. In 1998, LISC provided the seed capital for an initial investment in what is now the Community Development Trust (CDT).

LIMAC/CDT spun off from LISC with the public purpose of providing long-term capital to develop and preserve affordable housing. In May 1998, CDT closed a private placement offering that raised nearly $32 million from influential leaders in the field, many of whom still invest in CDT today.

Since its initial offering, CDT has raised $372 million and invested over $3.3 billion in 38,000 affordable housing units across the continental United States, Puerto Rico, and the U.S. Virgin Islands.

### National Community Development Initiative (NCDI)

We were well prepared to take advantage of a wonderful new opportunity from the Rockefeller Foundation that emerged just at the right time. We were gaining on our ambitious financial diversification goals, but we had no idea that a huge advance was coming our way in one giant step.

In a lucky stroke for the community development field, it turned out that the Rockefeller Foundation's new president, Peter Goldmark, Jr., wanted to diversify the Foundation's primarily international portfolio by adding a significant domestic focus and program.

A perpetual fountain of innovation in urban policy, Peter was no stranger to the merits of a grassroots community development strategy. He knew that scale mattered. Peter joined New York Governor John Carey's administration in his early thirties and became CEO of the Port Authority of New York and New Jersey at age thirty-five. He was also a founding board member of LISC.

Peter came up with the idea to accelerate the scale of community development corporations by leveraging the relationships of existing intermediary organizations, primarily LISC and Enterprise Community Partners. The National Community Development Initiative (NCDI) was officially launched in 1991 as a $60 million, three-year pilot program funded by the Rockefeller Foundation, seven additional private foundations, and one corporation.[6] At the time, it was the biggest alliance of private foundations coming together to do something significant, in this case to make a deep and abiding commitment to community development. NCDI's simple and elegant purpose was to pool significant grant resources and coordinate them with federal and private financing.

NCDI brought new, large sources of funds into the community development world, making staggering amounts of flexible resources available to communities where there were few sources of support. LISC was the lead intermediary, positioned to deliver new discretionary resources to the core group of cities that had signed on for "the grand bargain."

After a decade at Rockefeller, Peter headed to Europe to lead the *International Herald Tribune*, followed by deep focus on advocacy in the U.S. to address climate change issues. I highlight this aspect of Peter's career pathway because we've made a strong case in this book for pursuing careers that capture both public and private opportunities. Peter's story offers a powerful example of this trajectory.

## Comprehensive Approaches to Community Development

Even though LISC had decided to "go big" on housing as the focus of our work in the late 1980s, our local groups insisted that they were interested in continuing to work in other areas beyond housing. One of LISC's "secret sauces" in growing the entire enterprise was to start small locally and then scale nationally. From its earliest days, LISC was true to its name, taking inspiration for solutions from local communities. In my mid-to-late chapter at LISC in the 1990s, we experimented with a broader agenda including public safety, daycare, supermarkets, and rural programming.

During its formative years, LISC was all about urban places. Gradually, we began to realize that the people in Congress who were the most important to federal policy and funding decisions were largely from rural states. Sandy Rosenblith, who was one of LISC's original eight staff members working out of a Washington D.C. office, used to say "Paul, all states have two senators. Pay attention to the power base." The official Rural LISC program launched in 1995 with Sandy as its founding director. Over a period of nearly thirty years, Rural LISC has grown to partner with more than 140 rural community-based organizations and several

---

We deliberately launched a whole set of experiments to see if the LISC model could have the same impact in other areas as it had on housing. We tried some things that didn't work, but most things that emerged from LISC at the national level were actually pretty successful.

—Andy Ditton, former LISC executive and retired Citi managing director

---

> It is the first time in Massachusetts...that the giant social welfare agency [United Way] has contributed to the creation of housing...[F]unds are to be used for so-called 'core funding' to increase the staff strength and sophistication of community groups and, in so doing, enhance their capacity to create housing.
>
> —*Boston Globe*, "United Way pledges $1.8m for housing" (1987)

intermediaries. Their work spans more than 2,400 counties in forty-nine states and Puerto Rico.

One big idea that proved to be quite successful was to build the capacity of CDCs by providing operating support. CDCs were managing mammoth real estate projects with limited organizational capacity. Working with Bob Wadsworth at the Boston Foundation, Carol Glazer created the Neighborhood Development Support Collaborative (NDSC), the first initiative of its kind in the community development sector. It was modeled after the National Arts Stabilization Fund that rewarded organizations for strengthening their balance sheets, for performance and growth. NDSC was very successful and caught on with other LISC programs across the country whose directors came to Boston to learn how to replicate Boston's model.

The idea of capacity building also caught on with the federal government at HUD. The program known as "Section 4" supplies on average $35 million a year for capacity building, nearly half of which is awarded to LISC for distribution to its communities. This is a classic example of local innovation having national impact.

CDCs and housing nonprofits were not evenly deployed across the country. They were mostly a Northeast/Midwest phenomenon. We hired a remarkable guy as our head of community organizing, Mike Eichler. His mission was to help more CDCs form in mostly southeastern and some western cities. Eichler had incredible people skills. We stayed the course with this strategy for quite a few years and did form several new organizations. But for the most part, they didn't last. We didn't unlock the mystery of how to make the CDC approach work in the south. I don't have the answer. It's something to ponder. We had high hopes for the organizing effort, but it was largely disappointing.

## The Retail Initiative:
## Supermarkets, Shopping Centers, and Commercial Corridors

In the area of affordable housing, over a period of fifteen years, LISC had worked out effective delivery systems and ways to blend public and private financing at scale. Our question in the mid-1990s was whether these housing systems and financing mechanisms could be applied successfully to commercial projects.

We decided to make a big bet on bringing major supermarkets back to the inner city. In our view, this was a compelling place to begin a new experiment for the next generation of LISC's growth and relevance. Neighborhoods experiencing "food deserts" were literally hungry for a convenient and affordable source of quality food. We thought if we could help communities attract supermarkets, they could also create good jobs for residents, generate other businesses to support the supermarket anchor, and generally increase community vitality.

At LISC, we were convinced that supermarkets and neighborhood retail strips that had fallen into very bad condition had to come up with a new approach. Developers and supermarkets had long avoided inner-city communities. Neighborhood commercial districts weren't going to supply basic functions, but they could do something useful for the community. We were among the first organizations to observe this trend and opportunity. We hoped there was going to be another big LISC affiliate that we could spawn to develop supermarkets.

Our biggest, most successful, supermarket story took place in Harlem. But first we had to help shift the community's power dynamics and create a community development corporation capable of taking the lead on such an ambitious project. The story of how we did this had a huge impact on me personally and created friendships that I cherish to this day.

We had a very large LISC program in New York City. Our involvement in New York—which started before I got there with a special project grant for the South Bronx from the Ford Foundation—created some hard feelings that Harlem was not getting the same kind of support for development as the South Bronx. At the time, there weren't any CDCs in Harlem. There was a political machine that controlled everything in Harlem, including what got developed. There was the Harlem Urban Development Corporation (HUDC), a lackluster quasi-public entity that took up all the oxygen in the room. You couldn't get anything going without viable CDCs in the context of this unproductive public-private partnership.

We had already developed a strong working relationship with the City of New York and deputy chief of housing, Mark Willis. He met with us and said, "LISC has to get involved in Harlem. We're getting killed up there. Would you guys be willing to undertake an exploration as to whether a new CDC could be formed?" We agreed to do that, but I'm thinking, "How the hell do we get away with that in such a political environment?"

We went up to Harlem and met with Donald Cogsville, then head of the HUDC. His first question was "Paul, I'd like to know what you intend for our community." I thought to myself, "I wasn't born yesterday," so I said aloud, "We're not going to do anything that the community doesn't support, and that will basically determine our plan."

That approach worked! We formed a CDC in 1989, led by the Rev. Calvin Butts, which became the Abyssinian Development Corporation—an extraordinary group—and several other Harlem groups, a few of which are still around. Using the same formula I had used while working for Kevin White in Boston, we got people to calm down so we could create the new CDC and shift power within the community. We moved quietly and went about our business. The Harlem Urban Development Corporation folded several years later, replaced by a *bona fide* CDC. We had exposed the fact that HUDC wasn't doing anything for the community.

Then there was Darren Walker, himself already a one-man network of connections. Darren was the second in command of the newly formed Abyssinian CDC (and now president of the Ford Foundation). Fast forward, years go by, and Abyssinian and others are doing a great job. The neighborhood went from worst to first in New York.

One of the things we were keenly involved in developing was what the community desperately wanted: a supermarket in the heart of Harlem to anchor what everybody hoped would be a new Harlem Renaissance in the late 20th century. We bought into that vision and spent an enormous amount of time helping to make it happen.

One of Mayor Rudy Giuliani's big promises was to bring big box retail into the city. A supermarket would fit the definition of big box retail at the time, so Giuliani thought that maybe on substance he ought to support this effort. Then of course the small bodegas were very upset. They feared that the supermarkets were going to kill their business. They mounted a spirited (and almost successful) campaign to overturn the supermarket plan. In an about-face, even though it was contrary to his position on big box, Giuliani opposed the new supermarket because of the bodegas' campaign.

The supermarket plan could not go forward without Giuliani's approval. Everything was set to go, but Giuliani was under enormous public pressure because of his "big box" stance. So I became personally involved in the situation (even though I typically didn't get deeply involved in many local projects). This became my baby, not because I wanted it, but because it was important to LISC and to New York.

The do-or-die moment came when Rev. Butts got a call from Giuliani's economic development director, directing him to come to a meeting at two o'clock that afternoon. (At the time, Rev. Butts was pastor of the Abyssinian Baptist Church and the powerful head of its CDC.) The so-called invitation was terse, bordering on threatening: "The mayor has two draft press releases in his possession. One reluctantly cancels the project. The other confers his approval and goes forward. But in order for you to get Giuliani's approval, you must include a piece of the partnership for an

81

Hispanic group. They'll get part of the deal, a minor part, but part of the deal nonetheless."

Rev. Butts was enraged that his group was being treated like this by the mayor, commanded to show up to consider two diametrically opposed press releases. He couldn't have been more insulted. I was there for this meeting. In fact, the mayor insisted that I be there. The debate went back and forth. Rev. Butts was so visibly enraged by the whole thing that he tried to leave the meeting. He got up, and as he tried to walk out, I literally grabbed him and physically prevented him from leaving. I put my arms around him and just kept saying, "Calvin, look at the deal. I know you have every right to be insulted. It's outrageous. But look at the deal. We got it!"

As it turned out, the Hispanic part of the deal was just a ploy on the mayor's part. In fact, it was never acted upon. The further irony is that the supermarket doesn't exist either. That first market was superseded by much bigger "big box" supermarkets.

But what it did for Harlem was unleash development on 125th Street. It was like taking the stopper out of the bottle. And it earned me the friendship of Darren Walker and Rev. Calvin Butts.

The Retail Initiative got off to a great start, and we had high hopes for it. We did a few deals, including a 78,000 square foot shopping center in Chicago (1997) anchored by a supermarket and drug store that is still in business today. It was the first new shopping center in Chicago's Kenwood neighborhood in over fifty years.

But then a couple of things happened that caused us to reverse course. One is that the complex deals we got involved in took way too long to complete, and we didn't have the capital to keep them going. We only financed three or four projects where LISC really made a difference. In the end, we succeeded in raising the issue, and we did a few deals, but we couldn't make the initiative work as more than a one-off kind of thing. We continued to support supermarkets and CDC partnerships with supermarkets, but we didn't have the same success we had experienced with the other affiliates in making it into an enterprise.

(Left to right) Donna Smither, People's Housing, Chicago Mayor Richard M. Daley, and Paul Grogan.

## Closing Thoughts on LISC: Building the National Infrastructure to Support Community Development

With such great foresight, the Ford Foundation created LISC in 1979 as an intermediary to channel capital and build the capacity of CDCs to revitalize urban America. In so many ways, it was implausible to think that nearly forty years ago LISC could parlay a few local hidden gems from cities like Boston, Chicago, and New York into a sustainable national network of programs. It was an even greater reach of vision and ambition to think that the federal policy machine could be reinvigorated by passage of the Low Income Housing Tax Credit, or that LISC would be able to take first-mover advantage to fill a gap in the private market with the National Equity Fund and as a result initiate an explosion of new affordable housing.

What is most remarkable is not so much the beginning of that journey, but rather that groundwork laid in the 1980s has led to astounding results in affordable housing production and preservation. We all should acknowledge that housing is not the only aspect of community development that warrants attention and investment, but it is the biggest catalyst for change and a dynamic accelerator.

Taken together, the more than $30 billion in investments made since 1979 through the end of 2022 by LISC (the parent company), its affiliate the National Equity Fund (1987), and a LISC spin-off organization called the Community Development Trust (1999), have made it possible to produce more than 525,000 units of affordable housing across the continental United States, Puerto Rico, and the Virgin Islands.

LISC's work helped to inspire passage of the Community Development Financial Institution (CDFI) Act in 1994. We provided a significant proof point that investing in neighborhoods, and community development corporations, was not only safe but wise. More and more organizations at local, state, and national levels have become certified as CDFIs, spreading the impact beyond our wildest dreams.

As important, the brilliant young LISC team went on to key leadership positions across philanthropy, nonprofit organizations, and the private sector that have helped to improve the lives of millions of Americans in ways that have cascaded beyond LISC. This generation of leaders provided even more evidence of an emerging ecosystem and pathway to a career in community development.

We took a moment and helped to make it a movement.

# — 5 —

# Repairing a Frayed Town/Gown Relationship

HARVARD UNIVERSITY AND THE CITY OF BOSTON

1999-2001

In 1998, after thirteen years as CEO of LISC, I was seriously considering a move back to Boston. I had three young boys, and my travel schedule was taking a toll. I wanted more precious time with them.

## Heading Back to Boston

That September, I got a call from Jackie O'Neill, who was on the Harvard president's staff, and who actually understood the city and its politics. Her overture was followed by a call from President Neil Rudenstine to ask whether I would be willing to talk with him about joining Harvard in an external affairs position to help address town/gown challenges. I went up to Boston where the president, some of the key deans, and a few major donors put on a full-court press to get me to do this job.

They knew I had a very good relationship with Mayor Tom Menino— he and I went back nearly two decades to my work for the City of Boston. From my standpoint, the basic thing you have to do to be successful in public service is build relationships based on trust and openness. Tom Menino and I had done that in the late 1970s and 1980s around our shared

Harvard University, March 26, 2001. *Photo by Evan Richman. © Boston Globe.*

interest in Community Schools, CDCs, and the Main Streets program. We had bonded.

I went back to New York, and a day later they offered me the job. Economically, it made no sense. I was asked to take a substantial cut in salary and benefits. My primary concern was that I was moving into a staff role after a decade and a half of being a CEO. Would the dynamics work? But work/life balance was my priority. Within the space of a very short time—a couple of weeks—I accepted Harvard's offer to come back to Boston and work not only to get Harvard out of its current trouble with the City of Boston but also put things in place that would prevent it from happening in the future.

I agreed to do it, but with less enthusiasm than I've had about other jobs in my life. I left LISC and joined Harvard as the Vice President for Government, Community, and Public Affairs, and also secured a Harvard Business School teaching appointment as a senior lecturer. It seemed I would be skipping the step of attending business school!

It took a few months to wrap things up in New York and move my family to Boston. But by January 1999, I was ready to jump in full steam ahead to tackle the laser-focused priority for which Harvard President Neil Rudenstine had hired me: fix the university's problems working with the City of Boston. I began to build an external affairs staff including Lauren Louison, who had been my chief of staff at the City of Boston's NDEA, and Travis McCready, who I hired to be director of community relations.

## Carson Beach Redux

When I returned to Boston in 1998, I would take my sons around the city as I got reacquainted and we became Bostonians. As noted in my introduction to *The Good City* several years later, moving to New York "had the added benefit of giving me an 'outsider's' view of Boston's turnaround. I was

> Decades later, [Rev. Miniard] Culpepper looks back at the 1975 beach protest as a victory for Boston's Black community. 'Whenever I ride by there and I see Black people and White people on the beach and enjoying the beach, it reminds me of how much we fought for them to be able to enjoy that beach today,' he said. Today, the sandy stretch along Dorchester Bay draws a more diverse crowd.
>
> —*Boston Globe*, "45 Years Ago Black Protesters Sought to Desegregate Carson Beach" (2020)

stunned by the changes—almost all positive—that I saw in the city. The old tribalism seemed to have waned, leaving a forward-looking city more permeable, tolerant, and human than the one I remembered. The city had certainly changed, and maybe it took being away for a while to recognize just how much."[7]

One of the things I was curious about all these years later was Carson Beach. On a sunny Sunday afternoon, we headed over to the Dorchester and South Boston area. I didn't have a heavy political agenda. I was just mildly curious about what had gone on there in the intervening years.

I was absolutely stunned by what I saw—throngs of people strolling along, eating hot dogs, throwing Frisbees, playing touch football. In other words, Carson Beach was looking every bit as you would expect a healthy community to look. It had become a completely racially diverse park. In fact, there were interracial couples strolling together.

But it was mind blowing if you knew about, or had lived through, my experience in the mid-1970s. It was as if I'd been Rip Van Winkle or something like it, coming out of my sleep and into this wonderful beachfront park that offers recreation amenities to everyone.

It's truly remarkable—but actually no accident—that Boston's many waterfront beaches finally came out of a long period of neglect reflecting the demographics of the time and the fact that all population growth was

Carson Beach, August 12, 2023. © *Boston Globe*.

in the suburbs. The beaches existed, but they were in terrible condition and not really used. Save the Harbor/Save the Bay was founded in 1986 to clean up the harbor and make it safe for future generations. By the time I arrived back in Boston in 1998, the work was well under way, with funding from the Boston Foundation, to lift up the status of Boston's city beaches.

## Sizing up the Town/Gown Fracture

For many years before my arrival back in Boston, the relationship between Harvard University and the City of Boston had been very tense. Part of the problem was that Harvard thought of itself as a Cambridge institution, yet three of its most prestigious schools—Harvard Business School, Harvard Medical School, and Harvard School of Public Health—were in Boston. The relationship was not so much negative as it was uninformed. Mayor Tom Menino and Harvard President Neil Rudenstine had never even met in person, despite the fact that both men had been in their respective positions for more than five years.

The central town/gown issue that erupted in 1997 revolved around Harvard's land acquisitions in Allston, its adjacent Boston neighborhood. Rudenstine's predecessor, Derek Bok, had recognized a decade earlier that the Harvard campus footprint could not expand indefinitely in Cambridge. The fact that Bok had hired a real estate firm as a proxy to secretly buy up commercial and industrial properties in Allston became front page news. At one point, Mayor Menino accused Harvard of demonstrating the "highest level of arrogance" for secretly snapping up fifty-two acres of property in Allston, a perspective that also made headline news in Boston.

But beyond this precipitating incident, there was long-running resentment by Boston politicians about things like tax exemptions for the nonprofit institution and land ownership disputes. This is not uncommon in cities that are host to major universities. Town/gown relationships are typically tense, but they can be repaired. The situation can be viewed as two sides of a coin: universities and medical systems are job generators on the one hand, but they also create municipal revenue losses due to tax-exempt status. That is the entire basis for local payment-in-lieu-of-taxes (PILOT) programs.

About two years into this most intense period of negotiations surrounding PILOT payments and property acquisition in Allston, several major donors went to President Rudenstine and said, "You need to get somebody on your team who can find Hyde Park in the rain"—a reference to the working-class neighborhood that was Mayor Menino's home. Harvard needed to hire somebody with strong political connections to Boston. It was a void in Harvard's leadership. The university's external affairs staff was focused entirely on Washington D.C.

## Breaking the Town/Gown Logjam

For many years, Harvard had tried in vain to get Mayor Tom Menino's approval to acquire a giant parcel of vacant industrial land—over fifty acres—in nearby Allston. Although some smaller parcels had been quietly purchased over the previous decade, this massive parcel was a huge obstacle to future development. Harvard's goal was to create an exemplary science campus five minutes from the main campus in Cambridge.

Leveraging my long relationship with Mayor Menino, we persuaded him to approve a deal calling for Harvard to pay $40 million over twenty years to Boston in exchange for the city's approval to move forward with development-ready projects at the business school. This marked a turning point in the city's relationship with the world's wealthiest university and set

Boston Mayor Tom Menino and Paul Grogan, circa 1999.

the stage to make the purchase of additional Allston property feasible for university expansion.

The cash component of the agreement had multiple dimensions. First was a 45% increase in PILOT payments that Harvard had been making at the same level since 1975. Next was a pair of housing agreements: build 288 units of student housing on Harvard's Allston campus and add 554 units of housing for graduate students. And finally, the deal included $300,000 in linkage payments to be used for job training projects and low-cost housing in Allston-Brighton. By this time, Boston's innovation of linkage two decades earlier—which was developed during my tenure as a municipal employee—had become a permanent requirement. Much like the federal Low Income Housing Tax Credit, municipal linkage was a solid policy mechanism to help pay for affordable housing and related benefits.

On the day the deal was signed, August 25, 1999, the front-page lead story and an editorial in the *Globe* endorsed the Harvard initiative and praised Mayor Menino for approving the acquisition and a PILOT agreement. I was scheduled to address the agreement at a meeting of the Harvard Corporation and passed out copies of this editorial blessing by the *Boston Globe*. They couldn't believe it. It was viewed at the time as miraculous that we had done this. Everybody was so used to criticism from the *Globe* and community groups. Harvard's a big target. They were used to taking shots and getting pummeled.

Being at Harvard is incredibly fascinating even on bad days. There's nothing like it. The combination of talent, money, capacity, fire power, and ambition at that place is really staggering. That moment vindicated my decision to come to Harvard. I had a front row seat at the pinnacle of power in American higher education.

But I have to say, even though I was only there for three years, it ended up being a great experience from all sorts of standpoints. Even before the deal was signed, I received a personal hand-written letter of gratitude from President Rudenstine: "In your brief few months at Harvard, you have already made so clear, positive and deep a contribution, that everyone who

> Slowly, trust is rebuilding between the people of Allston and Harvard. Some of the credit belongs to Paul Grogan, a respected community development expert who took over in January as Harvard's vice president for government and community affairs. Grogan enjoys the respect of local officials.
>
> —*Boston Globe*, "What Harvard Owes to Allston" (1999)

has worked with you perceives—and appreciates—what you have achieved, and achieved so quickly. Thank you for your constant help, your advice, your new ideas, and your extraordinary effectiveness."

Most importantly, we got the job done. That overshadowed everything else.

Part of how we got it done can be attributed to what was going on in university-community relations all over the country. We'd arrived at a point nationally where people in cities everywhere were in real distress in a period of great economic uncertainty. We looked to other cities with major universities for lessons in how to create a strong relationship with city hall. We looked to University of Pennsylvania in Philadelphia and Trinity College in Hartford for ideas that might work for Harvard. Political leaders came to realize slowly that universities and hospitals could be counted on as stationary economic assets. They're not going to be leaving. It was the genesis of the "eds and meds" competitive strategy in most major cities.

Perhaps ironically, because there had been so many corporate mergers and acquisitions and loss of civic leadership, I could make the case to the mayor that real job creation would be coming from the universities, not necessarily from the business community. Forward thinking university leaders saw opportunities for partnership, working together with business and government to revive communities, rather than taking a defensive position to protect campuses from a declining surrounding city. Strategically, the relationship between town and gown could benefit both parties. A new concept of mutual self-interest began to take hold, dramatically so in Boston with the Harvard deal.

Because I was at a fairly senior level, I had a protected position for a while—and it's hard to have a protected position at Harvard. Everybody gets into everybody else's business. It's one of those kinds of places. I had been granted almost complete autonomy to get this deal done. A story by journalist Steve Bailey that ran in the *Boston Globe* on July 5, 2000, eighteen months after I arrived, nailed the double-edged sword of being in a privileged position to quickly accomplish a challenging goal:

> Could Paul Grogan be just warming up? Since landing back in Boston eighteen months ago, Grogan has been busy. Job one: repairing Harvard's questionable—to be kind—relationship with its neighbors on both sides of the Charles…Grogan was also recruited last year by Tom Menino to negotiate a settlement with the U.S. Department of Housing and Urban Development. In the do-or-die hours of the drive to get a new Fenway Park built, Grogan is one of the mayor's key negotiators at the bargaining table. At forty-nine, Grogan is in danger of becoming that most inviting of targets in this town: a rising star. Worse still, a rising star in that small, bitchy community that is Harvard University…Grogan's too-smooth style, monogrammed shirts, and framed newspaper articles of himself on his office walls have already been noted by real Harvardians, and not favorably.

## Economic Impact | Affordable Housing | After School Programs

As the real estate and PILOT negotiations were unfolding, we decided to conduct an economic impact study as part of our efforts to improve strained relationships with the community. "Harvard and the Community," published in late September 1999, documented Harvard's $2 billion annual economic impact on Greater Boston. It dispelled the widely held impression that Harvard wasn't doing anything for the community. We were also able to make the case that the jobs of the future—in fact, the whole trend of the economy—was going to be in the areas of pharma and technology.

Communities like Boston that have a concentration of institutions of higher education were well equipped to compete in the new "knowledge economy." Just by being themselves, major research universities had then, and continue to have, an immense economic impact. But what if business, government, and these universities were joined in a strategic effort to leverage these assets even more? In a similar vein, many urban colleges and universities were newly engaged in trying to improve their surrounding neighborhoods. In Boston, our motivator has been competitive advantage.

In November 1999, Harvard approved my idea for a "20-20-2000" initiative based on a new $20 million investment to provide low-interest loans to build affordable housing in Cambridge and Boston. Boston Community Capital, Boston LISC, and the Cambridge Affordable Housing Trust were tapped to implement the fund. The $20 million fund, launched in 2000, was loaned over twenty years at an incredibly low two per cent interest rate. In its first decade, the fund helped to build or renovate 4,350 units of affordable housing, which represented 17% of all affordable housing in those two cities. In addition to the loans, Harvard committed $1 million for one-time grants to nonprofits working in the housing space. In the first year, the Housing Improvement Program awarded $605,000 to thirteen agencies. (Jumping ahead to 2020, this program was renewed for an additional $20 million.)

At that time, the *Boston Globe* wrote: "Believed to be the most significant investment in community development by any university in the nation, the initiative provides an unusual partnership to link the university's brainpower to the resources." In a previous era, a lot of universities sat around while their neighborhoods deteriorated around them. They didn't think it was their job to deal with these issues. Now they understand that it is.

The next year (2001), the focus of our community connections shifted to after school programs for kids. On March 15th, we announced a $23 million, five-year partnership called the "After School for All Partnership." After school programs were a priority for Mayor Menino. Chris Gabrieli, who currently chairs the Massachusetts Board of Education, chaired the mayor's task force. (Coincidentally, Chris was a member of the Boston Foundation board and served on the search committee that selected me as CEO.)

Harvard's commitment to the initiative was $5 million, matching the City of Boston's contribution. Nine other organizations, including United Way of Massachusetts Bay, the Robert Wood Johnson Foundation (RWJF), and the Boston Foundation, committed the remaining $18 million. Carol Glazer, my former VP at LISC who was at that time consulting with RWJF, was instrumental in helping me get the deal done.

## Celebrating Progress: *Comeback Cities*

At Harvard, I was free from the day-to-day challenges of running a large, national organization, which provided the opportunity for reflection about the unexpected and largely unheralded progress cities had made in the 1990s.

Harvard also encouraged me to maintain my ties to the world of cities and community development nationally. Particularly satisfying was continuing to serve on the board of the National Equity Fund, being elected board chair of the Community Development Trust, and joining the Knight Foundation board.

Harvard was also the perfect environment for reflection and writing. A little over a year after I left LISC to join Harvard, journalist Tony Proscio and I completed our book, *Comeback Cities: A Blueprint for the Revival of America's Urban Neighborhoods,* for publication in 2000.

In 1998, Tony and I had decided it was time to shout from the rooftops about the progress American cities were making to rebound from decades of physical blight, economic decline, and racial strife. While I was still CEO, we pitched the idea for *Comeback Cities* to the LISC board with this thesis: "The American city is rebounding—not just here and there, not just cosmetically but fundamentally." LISC had clearly been part of the solution. Shepherded by then-chairman Jake Mascotte, we were supported 100% by

Paul Grogan and Mayor Tom Menino at a *Comeback Cities* book launch party hosted by Harvard President Neil Rudenstine in the auditorium of the Boston Public Library.

the board and senior staff. LISC sponsored the publication of the book, and as such, benefited from royalties.

*Comeback Cities* was published at the mid-point of my tenure as a vice president at Harvard. With the most critical aspects of my work to restore town/gown relationships completed, I was encouraged by President Rudenstine to promote the book across the country. So off I went to speak at a series of more than thirty book launch events, hosted by community foundations and/or local LISC programs, to spread the gospel of urban revitalization.

I was prepared to be lucky: my extensive book launch tour garnered tremendous media attention across the country as it was leading me away from Harvard and toward the Boston Foundation!

With permission from Beacon Press, successor to the original publisher Westview Press, this excerpt from the Introduction and Conclusion to *Comeback Cities* is exactly what we wanted to say, then and now, about the

> In their new book, *Comeback Cities*, Paul Grogan and Tony Proscio describe some of the remarkable, even miraculous improvements that have occurred in previously devastated neighborhoods in Kansas City, New York, Chicago, Cleveland and other big cities across the country.
>
> —*The New York Times*, Op-Ed "In America" (2000)

rebirth of American cities at the turn of the century. For ease of reading, we condensed the excerpt to make our key points.

*Introduction*

Something different is happening. This evidence consists of four trends. Together they constitute a 'surprising convergence of positives' that seem to presage a broad inner-city recovery.

The first is the maturing of a huge, rapidly expanding grassroots revitalization movement in America. A second, related trend is the rebirth of functioning private markets in former wastelands where, until recently, the only vigorous market activity had been the drug trade. The third propellant of inner-city revival is dropping crime [rates]. Fourth, and finally, has been the unshackling of inner-city life from the giant bureaucracies that once dictated everything that happened there—in particular the welfare system, public housing authorities, and public schools.

Reviving markets, dropping crime rates, and deregulating public systems open vistas for the inner city not seen in nearly fifty years, before the great postwar exodus and decline. These new trends combine powerfully with the now-extensive grassroots revival efforts.

We argue throughout, and particularly in a concluding reflection, that there is plenty that the public and private sector can do to enlarge and accelerate those trends: to make the community development movement an even more potent force; to speed the recovery of inner-city economies; to sustain the recent drops in crime; and to ensure that deregulation of the inner city is successful.

Forging a healthy connection between what is working locally and what needs to be done nationally is one overarching ambition of this book.

### Conclusion: Seizing the Moment

What the United States seems most to be lacking as the twentieth century closes [is] confidence that an urban rebound is achievable and worth the effort.

Some bounce was inevitable after so great a plunge—but a bounce shouldn't be mistaken for levitation. There's a curious problem with the 'natural bounce' theory: not all once-falling cities are rebounding alike.

Cities tell stories of intentional effort, intelligent public policy, and a stubborn confidence that inherited conditions and traditional methods can be changed dramatically and for the better, even when they are the work of isolated players not intentionally working together [yet] share a coherent rationale that links all four of the forces we have described: neighborhood-based development, private capital, public order, and deregulated or decentralized service systems.

By directing capital, profit incentives, and more effective social organization and services into neglected places, government and civic and community organizations can create an inviting environment for investors to develop local assets.

(Left to right) Harvard President Neil Rudenstine, Paul Grogan, and Boston Mayor
Tom Menino.

In other areas, public 'interference' in free markets has given birth
to some of the triumphs of American civilization, e.g., highways,
airports, bridges, military, basic research, secondary mortgage market, modern communications, the Internet.

Respecting market dynamics while injecting strategic incentives is
precisely what government is learning to do.

Although [these] forces...form a coherent set of ideas, they are not
yet being applied in an especially coherent way. They have mostly
arisen helter-skelter and separately. The very idea of an 'urban agenda' has lost its currency.

As a result, most self-respecting urbanists have lately shaken off
the 'urban policy' mantle altogether, in favor of the more visionary

(and vastly more complicated) study of 'metropolitan' or 'regional' issues—none of which has yet picked up much political traction.

What if by 'urban agenda' we came to mean a systematic, concerted application of the four elements we have outlined—letting neighborhood groups set and manage their own priorities; enforcing order and safety in public places; freeing market forces to rebuild what was abandoned or destroyed; and deregulating the critical public systems of education, housing, and social welfare? These four forces, thus far disconnected and haphazard, could finally make up a single blueprint for healthier neighborhoods and more prosperous cities.

## Harnessing the Power to Make a Difference: CEOs for Cities

Of particular importance to me as I made the move from New York back to Boston—and from LISC to Harvard and ultimately to the Boston Foundation—was heralding the power of an aligned business community and effective town/gown relationships to accelerate the pace of progress. My Harvard experience proved to be an extraordinary ephemeral case study that fueled my instinct for engagement in a collaborative national effort to leverage relationships and assets.

While still at Harvard, I was able to continue to play a leadership role in organizing a new venture called CEOs for Cities, a confederation of about forty big city mayors, business leaders, and university presidents committed to working together to build the economic competitiveness of cities. In 2001, Chicago Mayor Richard M. Daley and I worked together to create CEOs for Cities as a national nonprofit and forum designed to capture and share best practices and innovative efforts to improve urban economic competitiveness. The forum was organized around a multi-sector membership network composed of government, corporate, university, and nonprofit ex-

> By strengthening cities we are increasing the competitiveness of regions and enhancing the economic health of the nation. Using market-based reasoning to attract investment, CEOs for Cities is helping to change public perceptions of inner cities. They are harnessing the efforts and interests of public, private and nonprofit leaders, all of whom have a stake in increasing the vitality of inner cities, to help reveal the vast resources and untapped markets of the nation's urban centers. This means positive change for some of the country's most underdeveloped neighborhoods.
>
> —Jonathan F. Fanton, former president of the MacArthur Foundation

ecutives from major U.S. cities. Charles Ratner, CEO of Forest City Enterprises in Cleveland, Ohio, joined Mayor Daley as founding co-chair.

The vision of CEOs for Cities focused on four assets: connection, innovation, talent, and investment, which were branded together as City Vitals (ideas, benchmarks), City Clusters (networks of cross-sector leaders), and City Dividends (catalyst for collaboration and change).

We had a strong theory of action: cities are big enough to make an impact, and small enough to make things happen quickly, while Washington ponders and argues about partisan matters, tight budgets, and the lightening pace of global change. Cities and metropolitan areas can and should take control of their futures. In the words of Steve Jobs, the cities and regions that "tear down walls, build bridges, and light fires" will be the ones that change their futures.

The wisdom of our goals was rewarded early on (2002) with a $750,000 start-up grant from the John D. and Catherine T. MacArthur Foundation. The purpose of the three-year grant was to research urban land use reform and develop materials to help educate Congress about trends and opportunities in urban areas.

The original work of CEOs for Cities continues today under the aegis of Forward Cities.

## Closing Thoughts on Harvard University: Stay the Course Because All Good Things Take Time

When President Rudenstine announced he would retire, I wanted to plan my departure from Harvard around the same time. President Rudenstine and Mayor Menino had dramatically changed the relationship of the respective bodies they served by acknowledging that research universities drive urban economic growth in the 21st century. It is in everyone's best interest that these relationships be symbiotic, not confrontational.

During my time at Harvard, I gained great appreciation for the academy and all who worked there, but not enough to stay. While I knew for certain it

"For Paul—You have made wonderful contributions to Harvard—and to Boston and Cambridge—and the University will miss you greatly. All my best, Neil." 2001 Harvard Commencement.

was time to leave Harvard, I was just as certain that I wanted to stay in Boston. My boys were flourishing and Boston had become our forever home.

Fast forward to 2023, nearly a quarter century after that momentous day when the logjam between Harvard and the City was broken. The headline of the *Boston Globe's* June 19, 2023, business section shouted, "Harvard set to break ground on research campus." The lead paragraph announced, "Construction will begin this week in the first phase of Harvard's Enterprise Research Campus, a long-planned mixed-use development in Allston across Western Avenue from Harvard Business School." The vision for the property survived the twenty-four-year gap intact with the first phase plan in place by 2019. It presumably took most of that time warp to secure a developer and source of construction financing capable of delivering on a what has become a $750 million project.

# — 6 —

# Taking Community
# Philanthropy to Scale

## THE BOSTON FOUNDATION

### 2001-2021

Once again, fifteen years after joining LISC, the search firm Isaacson Miller held the keys to my career destiny.

The firm was hired to identify a successor to long-time Boston Foundation president Anna Faith Jones. By the time her retirement from the Boston Foundation ("the Foundation" or TBF) was announced, my work at Harvard had run its course. The big wins were behind me, and life at Harvard was settling into a typical bureaucratic mode. I wanted none of that. Plus, President Neil Rudenstine had announced his retirement from Harvard after a decade leading the university. I was about to join the ranks of ordinary mid-level vice presidents.

Yet again, luck was on my side. Not only was I ready to leave Harvard just as the Foundation was preparing to activate its leadership strategy, but my good friend and early mentor, Ira Jackson, was a member of the search committee. Timing matters!

This time I knew I was ready to jump into the pool of candidates to be vetted by Isaacson Miller. This was my pitch to the search firm in January 2001:

A large part of the appeal [of the Foundation] is that, unlike other charities, the size of a community foundation is not confined to investment results. They can be grown—and the Boston Foundation needs to grow very much larger than it is. I actually like to raise money. Perhaps as a consequence of having had to raise so much money in earlier jobs, I do have a deep interest in effective philanthropy. Philanthropy at its best is seed capital for dreams, risk capital that can instigate real change.

Boston is, like all cities today, in severe need of civic institutions that can convene, catalyze, and ultimately produce concerted efforts to attack the problems we face. Complicating this task is that the traditional infrastructure of locally based corporations is busy disappearing. It is no accident that the "Vault"[8] stopped meeting some years ago.

A community foundation is among the few institutions that has the potential to pull the new economy and the new Boston together. This will require that the Boston Foundation president be an adroit "boundary crosser"—a person with credibility and standing in diverse communities and in the public, private, and nonprofit sectors.

I am very impressed by the potential, for instance, of the Boston Indicators Project; but there must be a strategy to market this data and make it fundamental to the policy making process across the sectors.

The Boston Foundation was one of the first community foundations in the country. Like its peers from the early 20th century, the Foundation was formed as a trust, its endowment funds managed and controlled by Boston Safe Deposit and Trust Company. The founder was the president of the bank, which would remain the sole trustee bank until 1982, when four others were added. The founder's son, a young lawyer, drew up the legal papers and served as the Foundation's first director for almost three decades.

In a series of annual report introductions, Charles Rogerson was quite articulate about the need to attack the underlying causes of urban problems.

For much of their history, most community foundations have confined themselves to two primary sets of activities: growing and overseeing philanthropic assets on behalf of the community and serving as a major grantmaker to support vital nonprofits.

My predecessor, Anna Faith Jones, boldly led a major structural change in the foundation and its governance, legally breaking the trust and gally breaking the trust and

Paul S. Grogan, President and CEO, the Boston Foundation. *Photo by Richard Howard, courtesy of the Boston Foundation.*

creating in its place a modern fiduciary institution. This big change was in a sense a casualty of corporate America. The numbers of banks and other financial institutions were shrinking through industry consolidation. Most of the Boston Foundation's assets were held by one trustee bank, Boston Safe Deposit and Trust Company, making it possible to argue for breaking apart the resulting concentration of risk. She convinced all of the trust banks to give up control, making the case for independent governance and the Foundation's ability to craft its own investment program. But despite this natural context, it was nonetheless a bold undertaking for Anna Faith and the Foundation. It gave a larger, far more representative, body the freedom to be innovative.

This structural change set the stage for a new generation of thinking about the future. The Boston Foundation went from a Model T structure to

> "A place where transformative things can happen is when you find the sweet spot between a leader's skills and passions, a board and a staff's dreams and hopes, and the needs of a larger community.
>
> —Rev. Dr. Ray Hammond, former chair, the Boston Foundation

at least NASCAR, if not Formula One. What should TBF do with its new-found potential? Previously, pursuing big ideas was prevented—or at the very least made quite difficult—by the old structure.

There was a group of people on the TBF Board who shared a conviction that the Boston Foundation was not all it could be. Some referred to it as a "sleeping giant." While the Foundation had done good things and made good grants, a lot more could be done to leverage the assets and resources of the Foundation to move the community forward.

What the Board envisioned was a real departure from what had gone before. Despite Anna Faith's brilliant, groundbreaking work to gain control over the Foundation's investments and assets, she was hesitant about being in the public eye and making speeches. The group of Board members who wanted change started casting about: Who could be that new person who would introduce the Foundation to a broader audience and put it at the center of civic life in Boston?

The key characteristics of the new leader the Board was looking for included externally oriented, willing to delegate management of the complex organization to be an active civic leader, experienced and comfortable with the public sector, and diplomacy skills.

There was a highly qualified internal candidate, but a fairly consistent view began to prevail that the Foundation needed to pursue a larger vision of what a community foundation could be. Because I had worked for Mayors Kevin White and Ray Flynn, worked closely with Boston leadership while I was the CEO of LISC, and had developed a good relationship with Mayor

Paul Grogan against a backdrop of the Charles River and downtown Boston. © *Boston Globe, May 14, 2001. Photo by Suzanne Kreiter.*

Tom Menino, I knew all the players and had a good sense of what could be done. I came prepared to my interview with a couple of yellow legal pads that I had completely filled up with the outlines of a plan for civic engagement. This became my presentation to the search committee. I was told afterwards by some directors that my interview presentation just blew everybody away with so much of what they wanted to see happen in the future.

They were looking for a fairly radical change. As one director later shared with me, during a board retreat they had asked themselves this question: is TBF all that it can be? The answer was no from the majority of the board members. They were looking for visibility, influence, and much more aggressive fundraising. They were looking for all the things that I had done in my previous positions. But at the same time, their vision was vague. They wanted change but didn't have any details worked out to transform the Boston Foundation. They would leave that to me.

Our ambitions were a match. I joined the Boston Foundation in June 2001.

## Transforming the Boston Foundation: Civic Leadership

As I described in Chapter 3, I'm a big fan of the "one hundred-day" approach to quickly laying out a vision for the future of an organization. It worked well at LISC, so I repeated the exercise at the Boston Foundation. One hundred days after I took over as CEO, we laid out our vision for how we would develop a toolbox that went way beyond what we could achieve just with our own grants. We asked ourselves: Are nonprofit grantees really doing good things with TBF's money, and can we prove it? Can we be more than a grantmaker? Are we a financial institution? We could completely transform the institution and become influential and consequential to the future of Boston. We could attract resources from other sources. Moving from an institution that really wasn't that aggressive about fundraising, we wanted to grow, we wanted to make a bigger impact. Everything we did flowed directly from that vision.

I had a head start in developing a strategy to implement this vision. One source was my plan to replicate the successful strategy "triangle" I developed at LISC with Patty Foley: communications, public policy, and fundraising, powered by data. I was well prepared by that experience.

The second source was luck. Mary Jo Meisner came along just at the time I was asking how we were going to manifest this commitment to growth. She and I had actually met while I was still working at Harvard. She came to talk with me because she was interested in my government relations job! Despite being a journalist covering eastern Massachusetts, Mary Jo wasn't aware of the Boston Foundation. We bonded over our mutual affinity for

Boston's shortage of civic leadership appears to be easing in the Menino era.

—*Boston Globe*, Editorial: "Stepping to the Plate" (2002)

Mary Jo Meisner, Vice President for Communications, Community Relations and Public Affairs, with Paul Grogan. (Board Chair Rev. Ray Hammond on screen.) *Photo by Richard Howard, courtesy of the Boston Foundation.*

external affairs being central to bringing about change—the power of high visibility, awareness of issues, and how to use connections and collaboration. It was almost scary, that initial long conversation we had, how congruent our views were.

Getting her to join the staff at TBF was huge in terms of our being able to move quickly on the sketch of an agenda that I had laid out to the Board in my interview. Once I started the new job, I had to convince the Board to create a brand-new position, which I did at my second board meeting. After Travis McCready—who I brought with me from Harvard to be my chief of staff and corporate secretary, and later hired a third time to be my Vice President for Programs—Mary Jo was my first hire. She was "an unusual suspect." As a political campaigner and journalist, Mary Jo brought a lot to the equation. Even before starting the job, she wrote a seven-page memo on what the Foundation could become. That became the start of our new civic leadership toolkit.

## The Six Pillars of Civic Leadership:
## Data, Research, Convenings, Communications,
## Fundraising & Public Policy

We set out six elements as the initial components of a new profile to become a civic leadership institution: data, research, convenings, communications, fundraising, and public policy.

First was data. When I got to the Foundation, Charlotte Kahn was working on this little project that nobody really understood. It was as if she had been hidden in the attic since the project was started in 1997 as a partnership between the City of Boston and the Metropolitan Area Planning Council. That turned into the Boston Indicators Project. (We think it was the first civic indicators project in the world. Now they're quite popular.)

The rest of the foundation wasn't interested in the Indicators Project and wasn't paying any attention to it. I recognized that Charlotte's work could help us quickly put together the first element of our new vision. I gave a fresh look at the Indicators Project, and it became a force in our own work and in the community. We took the Indicators Project out of the attic and into the living room. Today Boston Indicators serves as the research center for the Boston Foundation.

Some people think the purpose of data in leadership is to beat up the opposition with stats and figures. At the Foundation, we were a lot more nuanced about how data served the purpose to validate or refute a thesis. Data in leadership is deeply tied to communications and public policy which, in combination, bring the data to life.

We wanted to encourage the use of data by our own example, and by funding a significant amount of research. That was the opening gambit of TBF's transformation: data and research. We started conducting our own research, cranking out one report after another, further shaping the type of data we needed to collect on a regular basis. This approach has almost unending leverage because it can be applied and reapplied to any issue.

> The Boston Foundation became a convener of people, a convener of ideas, a convener of communities. I saw TBF becoming the place to be, the place to discuss ideas, the place to share innovation, the place to share best practices, the place to share challenges and policy resources.
>
> —Vanessa Calderón-Rosado, president of IBA

Next came the convenings. We immediately put together a series of civic forums. About every four to six weeks, we convened panel discussions about the most important challenges facing the Greater Boston community. We covered a broad swath of policy and program issues. Scores of people—sometimes hundreds—would gather in a venue at the Foundation that had never been available to them before. We discovered that there was a tremendous hunger in the community for serious conversations about the future of the city and the region. There was no one really speaking to that possibility. There was the occasional report by the Federal Reserve, or even by the Boston Foundation. But it had no connection, no identity, to the rest of TBF's work, particularly our grantmaking. We gave it one. These discussions produced new, exciting challenges to the way policy makers conducted their business. The stars were lined up.

Many community foundations, including the Boston Foundation, often said that they were the best kept secrets in town. We designed a strategic communications and marketing plan to shine a bright light on everything new that we were doing. We knew our lack of visibility hurt the Foundation's efforts to attract new donors and to have the influence that we wanted. Our goal was to reposition the Foundation as a civic leader.

We started by talking more publicly about our unique role as a grantmaker, the Foundation's bread and butter since 1915. That's how people knew us best. One of the first things I did when I arrived—with the help of Barbara Hindley, TBF's unofficial historian and official writer and editor

Founders of The John LaWare Leadership Forum (2005-2013): (Left to right) John Hamill, former chairman and CEO of Sovereign Bank New England; Cathy Minehan, former president and CEO of the Federal Reserve Bank of Boston; and Paul Grogan. *Courtesy of the Boston Foundation.*

for many years—was to start to uncover the unknown history of the Foundation. We learned that the Boston Foundation had been, from the very beginning, receptive to new ideas and risk.

I learned about the crucial early support the Boston Foundation had provided to help to launch some of Greater Boston's most important and enduring institutions. This prestigious list includes WGBH TV (now GBH TV), Commonwealth Shakespeare Company, Boston Children's Chorus, Year Up, the Community Builders, the New England Aquarium, and so much more. The clean-up of Boston Harbor in the early 1980s—then one of the most polluted harbors in the country—was triggered by several zealous advocacy organizations and the Boston Foundation's timely support of Save the Harbor/Save the Bay (led by none other than Patty Foley my former VP at LISC!). This discovery led to an incredible brand called *There at the Beginning* which we used to illuminate the past and brighten the path of the nonprofit sector toward the future. During my nearly two decades at TBF, we helped more than sixty nonprofit organizations and initiatives get started.

Later we branded our data, research, and convening activities under the banner of *Understanding Boston*. We aimed to become the go-to place for information and action important to Boston's future. We got great help from the Boston press. Reporters were seeking information and strong leadership. As we gained momentum, one local journalist said, "the *Boston Globe* is Grogan's personal newsletter." We used to say, "We live on page one." While this may sound a bit glib in retrospect, it was very important to the Boston Foundation's fundraising strategy.

When I started at the Foundation, we had $700 million in total assets. The day I left, we had $1.7 billion and had given away nearly $2 billion. Just think what a great deal this is for a community, to move millions of dollars to the right place and then replenish it. Suffice to say, our fundraising was aggressive.

I started at the Foundation right as Fidelity Investments was experiencing tremendous success in attracting donor advised funds (DAFs), a relatively new and very popular philanthropic tool that engaged donors in the grantmaking process. And we're in Fidelity's hometown! Fidelity had the market share of donor advised funds in Boston. We were determined to turn that challenge into an opportunity.

One of the things I'm most proud of is achieving success in an area which I understood the least. I really didn't know anything about the whole donor piece of our work. I had to spend a lot of time understanding donors and donor advised funds. We had to ask ourselves 'should we even be in this donor advised fund business?' We had board retreats on this topic shortly after my arrival. It was an active option to exit the business, to make some sort of deal with Fidelity, and instead focus on what we could do with our discretionary resources. That idea did not win the day because I wanted to give DAFs a try.

The problem with making a judgment call at that time about being in the DAF business was that TBF hadn't really done a good job of it up to that point. But if you actually paid attention and did some of the right things, maybe the result would look very different. So we decided to give it a shot. It turned out to be incredible. Fidelity has continued to rack up substantial assets, but there was room for a distinctive offering. TBF is now raising over $100 million a year thanks to Kate Guedj, the Foundation's outstanding development vice president and her team. For us to be in Fidelity's headquarters city, and to be able to establish a thriving donor advised fund business—that's pretty amazing.

Now TBF is a legitimate player in the DAF world. I admit I was pleasantly surprised. It is my pleasure to share this quote from our interview with Darren Walker, president of the Ford Foundation: "Paul was a change master for community foundations right in the shadow of the biggest donor advised fund in the world, Fidelity."

What we thought would be the most controversial change in direction for the Foundation was becoming involved early on in public policy issues on a nonpartisan basis without jeopardizing the standing of the foundation. Public policy was the sixth plank of our transformation toolkit. Putting the communications function together with public policy turned out to be a very smart thing. We were able to attract tremendous talent in Keith Mahoney and the late Jim Rooney. It just so happened that there were some front-burner issues at the time calling for legislative solutions, for instance the expansion of charter schools. There was a ready opportunity to do something that would get people's attention and serve as an announcement that "there's a new kid in town," a new Boston Foundation. It's going to be different from now on.

# — 7 —

# Making the Transition
# from Tradition
# to Transformation

Initially, the Boston Foundation was a typical grantmaking institution where people were siloed in their departmental responsibilities. There wasn't much cross departmental ambition or conversation of any kind. I started insisting that we harness in concert all of the capacities of the Foundation: grantmaking, research, public policy, convening, fundraising. We had to create a discipline of focusing on every opportunity we could.

The business community learned a long time ago that the most effective way to lead an organization is to train people properly and then push authority and responsibility as far down the organization as you can. This was a completely new way to do business and I needed someone in the top grant making job who understood that we were more than a grantmaker. Once again, I was very lucky. All three of my program vice presidents—Robert Lewis, Jr., Travis McCready, and Orlando Watkins—were tremendous team players and had great influence on our transition from tradition to transformation.

I hired Robert Lewis, Jr., in 2007 as Vice President for Programs with the stated goal of bringing the Foundation closer to the community and bringing the community into the Foundation. Robert was well-known in Boston for his passion for youth development and nonprofit leadership, having served as the

A Trio of Boston Foundation Vice Presidents for Program: (Left to right) Orlando Watkins, Travis McCready, and Robert Lewis, Jr.

director of both the Boston Centers for Youth & Families (originally Community Schools) and City Year. Early in his tenure, Robert arranged a series of about twenty meetings in every neighborhood and invited me along to listen and to give a short talk. He packed these gatherings with community leaders. We found that neighborhood folks were hungry for a conversation with the leadership of one of the largest foundations in town.

StreetSafe was among the innovative programs we initiated during Robert's tenure that linked our data and research to a community need. StreetSafe was designed to help combat youth violence by hiring street workers to engage neighborhood resident influencers. In a great success story about spinning off a program to a permanent home, StreetSafe is now run by the Boston Police Department—a signature program designed to fund grassroots organizations that would otherwise not get connected to mainstream philanthropy.

StreetSafe convening. *Courtesy of the Boston Foundation.*

Robert's favorite story, which has become one of mine, is about a $3,000 grant we made to a barbershop.

A small Black-owned barbershop was giving out books, book bags, and free haircuts to encourage kids to go back to school each September. We provided funding to support the barber's efforts. The third year, we increased the grant to $7,500 and expanded to two more barbershops. Like all foundations, we weren't prepared to fund the program forever. After a few years, about twenty barbershops started raising money themselves and giving out books with free haircuts in every neighborhood. A very small $3,000 investment became one of the hottest things in Boston to kick off every school year. Sometimes it wasn't the big grants that really moved communities. It was the small grants, grassroots grants—grants based on belief and investment in people—that generated so much more impact.

On a very personal note, I want to recognize Robert's mentorship of my three boys. I mentioned previously that my decision to leave LISC was based on my desire to spend more time with my family, and sports was a tremendous part of the equation for my sons. They all were good ball players and were recruited by Robert to join the inner-city baseball team he founded and coached, the South End Astros. I rarely missed a game. My boys were among

> One of Paul's greatest talents and attributes was the ability to see the endgame and to have a clear vision of how to go from a traditional, to a transitional, to a transformational organization.
>
> —Ed Lloyd, former LISC CFO

the few White teenagers on the team. Their experience under Robert's leadership was life changing for them and a real joy for me.

We experimented with a variety of grantmaking approaches at TBF, but we didn't abandon what was clearly already working. An example is *Inquilinos Boricuas en Acción* (Boricua Tenants in Action, or IBA), which was formed in 1968 as a single-purpose organization when Puerto Rican residents of "Parcel 19" in Boston's South End neighborhood organized against displacement by the attempt to extend US Route 95 through their neighborhood.

When the City of Boston shifted its approach to neighborhood development, while I was the director of the Neighborhood Development and Employment Agency, we started funding the work of nonprofit CDCs like IBA. Later, when I was at LISC, we also supported IBA's affordable housing work. The organization's current president, Vanessa Calderón-Rosado, joined IBA in 2003 when I was just two years into my new role as president of the Boston Foundation. Vanessa and I have joked over the years that whatever job I had at the time, I would be sure to provide resources for IBA. Today IBA has developed nearly 670 units of affordable housing and provides supportive housing services. As a final note on our important friendship, we invited Vanessa to join TBF's Board in 2018.

In addition to the senior staff members I've already mentioned—Travis McCready, Mary Jo Meisner, Kate Guedj, Robert Lewis, Jr., Keith Mahoney, and Orlando Watkins—I also kept my eye out for top young talent eager to learn about philanthropy and be part of the team making a huge difference in Boston. Believe me when I say that the list is too long to mention everyone, but I do want to mention Stephen Chan as an exemplar of a young person who with great intentionality chose community service.

Stephen approached me to be his mentor as he was coming out of the John Gardner Fellowship in public service at Stanford University. I was intrigued because John Gardner was a friend of mine. (Among many great things, John was the founder of Common Cause and the Secretary of HEW under President Lyndon Johnson.) Stephen saw it as providing free labor. I saw it as an opportunity to send a message to young people that they are welcome in the civic sector.

I gave Stephen much more access and responsibility than he thought he was ready for. Sound familiar? That's what Mayor Kevin White did for me as a young professional. I adopted that approach in my own managerial style. If the Broadway hit *Hamilton* had opened forty years earlier, I could have used the famous line from Lin-Manuel Miranda's song that I was "in the room where it happens," as could Stephen. He went on to Harvard's Business School and Kennedy School, followed by a second fellowship from Harvard, to work in the Menino administration as a policy advisor. And then like a lucky penny, he bounced back to the Foundation for a second time at my invitation to be my chief of staff and to focus on execution of the next phase of our big vision.

## The Six Pillars in Action

With a new strategy for transformation firmly in place, we created the tools that would embody the "new" Boston Foundation. First and foremost, we needed a new source of funding to support the elements of the new toolkit that included adding data, research, convening, communications, fundraising, and public policy initiatives to our core grantmaking role. Piece by piece, we built out our strategy that, within a decade, began to demonstrate remarkable results.

The most important thing is how those six elements were viewed in relation to one another. A seminal piece written a decade into our change

## THE CHRONICLE OF
# PHILANTHROPY.

The Newspaper of the Nonprofit World     Volume XXIII, No. 14 • June 2, 2011

## GIVING
Gifts, Grants, and Good Works

# A Boston Fund Mixes Research and Advocacy With Writing Checks

RICK FRIEDMAN, FOR THE CHRONICLE

Paul S. Grogan, who has led the Boston Foundation for 10 years, is also a registered lobbyist with the state of Massachusetts.

By Ben Gose

BOSTON

WALK INTO THE LOBBY of the Boston Foundation, and the first thing you see is a computer screen listing that day's public meetings—perhaps a forum on immigration, housing, education, or some other aspect of life in Massachusetts.

On a spring Monday, 40 economists and others were here to share their views on trends in the local economy for a report the foundation is preparing.

The list of meetings hints at the transformation of the 96-year-old foundation in the decade that Paul S. Grogan has been at the helm.

Grant making is no longer the only thing the foundation is known for but just another tool for promoting change, just as is conducting research, gathering community leaders, and lobbying on issues like education and government efficiency.

Now many other leaders of community funds nationwide are following Boston's efforts by redefining themselves as leaders on key public-policy issues, not just pots of money. (See article below.)

But many of those efforts shy away from controversy, unlike the Boston Foundation, which has plunged with gusto into the rough-and-tumble world of influencing local government and politics. In the past 18 months, it has led a coalition that helped Massachusetts win a $250-million education prize in the federal Race to the Top competition; issued two reports critical of the state's Probation Department, helping prompt an investigation that led to its commissioner's resig-

Reprint of the *Chronicle of Philanthropy*, June 2, 2011. *Courtesy of the Boston Foundation.*

strategy by the *Chronicle of Philanthropy* (2011) underscored the credibility of our toolkit and transformation. Central to the story was the point that grantmaking had become a tool, not the central focus, activated alongside research, convening, and lobbying, and that other community foundation leaders were leaning into this new way of working. The article quoted me as saying "You can't solve any of the problems we care about without effective government," a lesson I had learned with deep conviction years earlier at the City of Boston, LISC, and Harvard University.

The next year (2012), I was invited to develop an essay for the Duke University Sanford School of Public Policy as the second in a series of papers on contemporary philanthropy. Called "Civic Leadership at the Boston Foundation, 2001–2012," the essay incorporated a chart laying out key elements of civic leadership and depicting changes made over a decade in a classic "old way/new way" configuration.

This is how the essay and the process of transformation at the Boston Foundation (TBF) was described by Ed Skloot, former president of the Surdna Foundation, who in 2012 was director of Duke's Center for Strategic Philanthropy and Civil Society. He praised the Boston Foundation for ushering in the transformation in how community foundations conduct their business, and encouraged contemporary foundations to follow Boston's lead:

> Paul's arrival at TBF more than a decade ago had ushered in a transformation in how the Foundation did its business. In research, analysis, policy advocacy, communications, outreach, and numerous other clusters of its work, the changes have been planned, organic, and effective. Today there is universal agreement that TBF is one of the most effective foundations in the country. [This essay] shows how contemporary community foundations can become more agile, energized, relevant, and, not least, consequential in their communities. It offers a rough guide for foundations willing to intentionally take up the challenges of staying relevant and forging positive social change.

| Civic Leadership Element | Tradition | Transformation |
|---|---|---|
| Approach to Community Change | Focus on good programs and quietly supporting community change-makers; passive, behind-the-scenes. | Mobilize business and community leaders to action on key city issues. Activist, vocal grantmaker and civic leader. |
| Data and Research | Use data or research on a specific topic for organizational decision-making. | Rely on data and commissioned research to reveal or highlight diverse mission-driven challenges. Distribute findings and recommendations widely to stakeholders and influencers. |
| Media | Avoid media attention. Quietly support community leaders who are involved in conversations in your organization's area(s) of concern. | Court media attention. Shape and drive the conversation about key issues in your organization's area(s) of concern. |
| Public Sector Engagement | No lobbyists on staff. Episodic engagement with the public sector on specific issues. | Lobbyists on staff. Consistent, organization-wide engagement with the public sector on all aspects of strategy. |
| Storytelling | Little attention to tracking and publicizing your organization's stories and achievements. | Elevation of stories and achievements for community and media attention. |
| Fundraising | Fundraising focus only on general operations and programs. | Fundraising focus expanded to include operations support for leadership activities and long-term resources. |
| Staff Capacity | Small staff focused on core administration, finance, and programs. | Expanding staff also focused on development, communications, community relations, and public affairs capacity. |
| Controversy | Avoid controversy and public disagreements. | Selectively engage with controversial issues. Public disagreements viewed as occasionally necessary for real change. |

Now, more than a decade later with a fresh eye on the material, I concluded that there are nuggets of wisdom within these elements of civic leadership for community foundations that can be applied to any organization in the nonprofit or public sector. I also recognized that this tradition-to-transformation construct could be a useful device to braid the threads of multiple priorities, in the case of the Boston Foundation, how community development and community philanthropy blend to become powerful drivers for civic progress.

Today's civic leaders stand on the broad shoulders of those who came before us. Understanding the back story, the historical context, is the first and most important step toward any exercise of institutional transformation. While past is not prologue, it is deeply informative, offering lessons and insights as dos and don'ts for the future.

With this broadened perspective in mind, in the chart on page 124, the "old way" is tradition and the "new way" is transformation. This construct recognizes the degree of ambition, hard work, and intentionality required to transform an organization.

## Civic Leadership Fund (2003)

We wanted to open the doors to the Foundation and make it inclusive, to design it as a convening place. The Civic Leadership Fund was one of my first significant fundraising initiatives. It was a campaign designed to engage individual and corporate donors at all levels to become stewards of the Foundation and the communities it served. We needed additional unrestricted resources if we were going to do new things in the civic leadership realm. It was going to cost something to ramp up research, communications, convenings, etc. The board was enamored with the concept of civic leadership. But how would we pay for it? The answer was to create a civic leadership fund as the new opportunity, a compelling case to raise money and engage new donors in the Foundation.

Everybody was on the same page that we needed to ramp up civic leadership, but I couldn't get the TBF Board to move on launching a campaign. We discussed the idea multiple times at board meetings. When it wasn't clear that there was going to be a positive conclusion to the proposal, Bob Glassman of Wainwright Bank put a $25,000 check on the table and said to his board colleagues, "match this."

We were able to launch a campaign starting with that commitment, but we also had to get a lot better at development, to forge a lot of new relationships. We were aided by broad receptivity to the idea of a community foundation being a civic leader. It's astounding how positively people responded to what could have been a very uncomfortable change. We raised a quarter of a million dollars the first year in small increments of one-, two-, and five-thousand-dollar donations. We tapped into a huge fraction of the potential donor community previously not available to us because donor advised funds were the only engaging option we had to offer. It became unthinkable for our Board members not to contribute financially.

When I got to the Foundation, there were only a couple of people on the Board who wrote modest checks to the Foundation annually. They weren't asked for any money, so there was zero tradition of the Board taking real responsibility for developing resources. I remember Rev. Dr. Ray Hammond saying when he was Board chair, "We're not doing this unless every Board member does something. We don't care how much it is." Everybody fell in line right away that first year. We got one hundred percent participation. Over the years, growing the Civic Leadership Fund has become a priority for TBF.

One of the reasons it was successful is that it gave us something to talk about other than endowments and donor advised funds. In a place like Boston, even if you were at the top of your game, only a tiny fraction of the donor market chose TBF. But this gave people who liked what we were doing a way to be helpful. That turned out to be a huge development coup. They loved the fact that they could write a small check and be listed as a donor. The Civic Leadership Fund became the donor leadership platform to which everyone wanted their names attached.

In my final year at the Foundation, we raised $3.8 million for the Civic Leadership Fund, completely unrestricted.

## Public Policy Powerhouse

$R$eal change in society is never free of conflict. That isn't how the world works. You don't all get around the table, hold hands and say, "Now we'll have civil rights for everybody." As I learned from Boston Mayor Kevin White, if you're not making people angry, you're not working on anything important.

The idea of taking on public policy issues, making it a feature of the organization's toolkit, gained currency during my first conversations with the Board. I couldn't imagine how we would solve big problems without engaging the public sector. As I said earlier, we built capacity by hiring Mary Jo Meisner and then

(Left to right) Paul Grogan and Governor Deval Patrick with Massachusetts Undersecretary for Housing & Community Development Tina Brooks, and State Senator Anthony Gallucio, circa 2010. *Courtesy of the Boston Foundation.*

What I got from my partnership with the Boston Foundation, with Paul, was cover. There was another thoughtful source of ideas, of studies that tested multiple ideas and conclusions, and had a point of view about why one idea was superior to the others that were out there. You had a sense that you weren't all alone in trying to make a difference.

—Former Massachusetts Governor Deval Patrick

---

> Systems aren't faceless creatures. They are actors with leaders and staff and many people you can influence to change behavior. There is a performance arc to leadership when it comes to system action and transformation. An organization like the Boston Foundation can serve as a bully pulpit and platform to mobilize change.
>
> —Stephen Chan, former fellow and chief of staff at the Boston Foundation

---

building out a muscular external affairs staff team. We started looking for opportunities to make policy changes that would help our grantees to be successful.

We had lots of skeptics. There was no low-hanging fruit, nor were there any easy wins. We did big public policy work—so surprising for a community foundation. We had to worry about how the public, especially our donors, would react. It was controversial, but it all worked. The community was broadly supportive as we had the best data, research, and the ability to get that covered by the media. I only got one letter from a donor criticizing our new direction, but he still stuck with TBF.

In the view of some, we became a public policy powerhouse. Here are five illustrative examples demonstrating the diversity of our work across arts and culture, K-12 education (charter schools), higher education (community colleges), health care financing reform, and affordable housing in which TBF was indispensable to policy change.

### Cultural Facilities Act (2006)

For more than twenty years, the Massachusetts legislature had been trying to pass a bill that would provide funding for arts and cultural facilities. The Boston Foundation and its partners led a process that got it done in a year.

TBF published a report called "Culture is our Common Wealth" in 2006. The research documented more than $1.1 billion in brick-and-mortar needs among arts and culture organizations. Based on this finding, TBF re-convened and chaired an existing steering committee in collaboration with the Massachusetts Cultural Council and MAASH (Massachusetts Alliance for Arts, Sciences, and Humanities).

That partnership led to the creation in 2006 of the state Cultural Facil-ities Fund as part of a larger economic stimulus bill during Governor Mitt Romney's administration. The Fund makes flexible grants to support the ac-quisition, design, repair, rehabilitation, renovation, expansion, or construc-tion of nonprofit cultural facilities statewide. Since inception, this perma-nent Fund has awarded nearly 1,400 grants totaling $162 million benefiting 525 organizations across the Commonwealth of Massachusetts.

It's not an overstatement to suggest that the Boston Foundation helped to redefine arts and cultural facilities as critical components of our Common-wealth's economic development strategy. These facilities are not only part of our state's culture and identity, they are part of our competitive advantage. When he succeeded Romney in 2007, Governor Deval Patrick sustained the state's commitment to cultural facilities. He was greeted by the "great reces-sion" of 2008-09, which gave the Commonwealth a chance to step back and reimagine the future by emphasizing the power of the innovation economy, including cultural opportunities for people who work in that sector and want to work in communities where there are vibrant cultural amenities.

### Education Reform (2009-10)

A great example of collaboration was our work on education reform legis-lation passed during Governor Deval Patrick's administration. It was called the Massachusetts Achievement Gap Act of 2010 and was the most signif-icant change to K-12 education in a decade, putting Massachusetts at the forefront of a national movement.

(Left to right) Paul Grogan; Kevin Andrews, chairman of the Massachusetts Charter Public School Association; and Representative Eugene O'Flaherty, Chelsea, Massachusetts. April 29, 2009. © *Boston Globe.*

Representatives of the teachers' union, charter schools, parents, business leaders, and education advocates were all making different pitches for reforming public schools, but most of the early arguments focused on what was right for the adults. I remember Governor Patrick saying that we should just focus on the kids, accept that all kids are not the same, and that there wouldn't be a singular solution.

After that, we started to work on a bill where everybody involved in the process made a contribution to developing a menu of ideas that could lead to meaningful outcomes for children. There would be competition for resources, and accountability for results. We were freed to innovate by the notion that we didn't have to be aligned around a single set of strategies. It wasn't just an easy way out of a disagreement; it was a radical way to think about meeting kids where they are and truly not leaving any child behind.

Everybody who had a stake in the outcome was in the room, at the table, and stayed there until the very end. We were able to overcome the inertia

OFFICE OF THE GOVERNOR
**COMMONWEALTH OF MASSACHUSETTS**
STATE HOUSE • BOSTON, MA 02133
(617) 725-4000

**DEVAL L. PATRICK**
GOVERNOR

**TIMOTHY P. MURRAY**
LIEUTENANT GOVERNOR

February 16, 2010

Mr. Paul Grogan
The Boston Foundation
75 Arlington Street, 10th Floor
Boston, MA 02116

Dear Mr. Grogan:

Belated but sincere thanks for all your good help on the education reform bill. You know how important these new tools will be in helping to close the achievement gap and letting more innovation flourish in public schools. We could not have come this far without you.

There is a broader lesson here about the good that comes when diverse leaders work together. I look forward to other successful collaborations with you in the future.

With gratitude,

*This was our finest hour!*

Deval

of self-interest. We did some very ambitious things, some of which were controversial, but the legislation passed and we got surprisingly good results.

One feature of the new law was lifting a cap on the number of charter schools that could be created at any one time. Another was a deep partnership with the Mayor of Boston, Tom Menino, to provide in-district charter schools and Innovation Schools, reforms that were at the heart of his 2010 re-election campaign. This innovative state law unlocked $250 million in federal funding under President Obama's historic Race to the Top initiative. As Governor Patrick said to me at the signing, "This was our finest hour."

The headline of a column in the *Boston Globe* that day read something like "Charter schools have a powerful new friend." Even though we weren't able to carry our success beyond an initial victory because the teachers' union opposed the idea, the early work we did in helping the governor to expand charter schools in 2010 was key to future education reform and better student outcomes.

### Municipal and State Healthcare Reform Legislation (2011)

Of all the issues we took on, this may be the most unusual. The issue of health coverage for municipal workers was viewed as a labor relations matter, not one ordinarily taken up by a community foundation. Our rationale for stepping boldly into this issue was the fact that the cost of municipal health care coverage was having a cascading and devastating impact on overall municipal budgets, eating away at funding for basic services, schools, infrastructure, etc. Municipal jobs were being cut.

Municipalities in Massachusetts were permitted to negotiate their own health plans. That was the home rule tradition starting as early as the American Revolution and codified in 1966. In the context of growing concerns about health care costs, the Boston Foundation played a role in exposing that the cost of municipal plans was 4-5% above normal cost inflation. Municipal unions had grown accustomed to asking for richer health plans as wage-increase concessions. In addition, individual municipalities did not

(Left to right) Paul Grogan; Dr. JudyAnn Bigby, former Massachusetts Secretary of Health; former Governor Deval Patrick; and Steven Hyman, M.D., former Harvard University Provost. *Courtesy of the Boston Foundation.*

have the staff to effectively manage these plans, adding to excessive costs. The issue quickly escalated beyond the particulars of expensive healthcare administration to how communities could sustain operations in the face of an enormous drain on resources.

We learned from our research that Massachusetts had a state plan which localities could join. The credibility of our research, highlighting the cost effectiveness of that state plan, and support from a broad coalition of mayors—all of whom had deep pro-labor *bona fides*—allowed us to propose a legislative solution. The new performance standard required municipalities to either meet the standard or join the state plan. Most cities could not meet the performance standard. We may have thought this kind of massive change was impossible at the time, but it worked.

Former Speaker of the House Robert DeLeo often referred to this matter as his favorite piece of legislation because of all it accomplished and because everybody won. While labor interests fought the legislation, at a closed-door caucus of House Democrats, DeLeo handed out copies of TBF's report and challenged his members to defy the logic of our suggested approach. TBF defined the issue more broadly such that it could be acted upon in a bipartisan vote of support. The potential positive impact was so huge it couldn't be ignored by anyone.

Within two years, nearly 40% of all towns in the Commonwealth began participating in the new state program and saving $175 million annually in healthcare costs—a number that has continued to grow over the past decade.

### Community Colleges (2011)

One of TBF's best examples of action-oriented research is a 2011 report called "The Case for Community Colleges: Aligning Higher Education and Workforce Needs in Massachusetts."

When we decided to take on community college reform, it was because they were mired in a narrow tradition as two-year colleges to prepare students to go on to four-year colleges. The thinking in other states at the time was that community colleges should become centerpieces of preparing the workforce for today and tomorrow. It was potentially a very different role.

TBF had experience with the workforce approach due to our engagement with Boston's remarkable teaching hospitals and their need for staff. After learning of their frustrations trying to navigate our community college system, TBF conducted a study that focused on how these institutions were meeting the needs of their students and potential employers. We also engaged with Governor Patrick, who showed interest in pursuing reform so long as we could provide a path forward.

The study made front page news. Its pointed recommendations included stabilizing funding for community colleges and strengthening the governance structure. This is how Mary Jo Meisner described the role of the Boston Foundation in changing a broken system of community colleges in Massachusetts:

We broke some eggs and took a lot of arrows trying to help fix the community college system, but it was the right thing to do, and it was important to student success and to the economy. We proposed a set of changes to the governance of community colleges, and also proposed to bring more state money to these institutions that were not viewed with respect or credibility in the education arena. That led to related efforts in workforce development opportunities for young people through Success Boston and other K-12 initiatives. If I had to name one powerful thing the Boston Foundation achieved, it was education and workforce development in the growing knowledge economy. We made clear that talent was our number one issue in the city.

We weren't sure what Governor Patrick intended to do as a result of the report, but when we attended his annual state-of-the-state address, we were pleasantly surprised that community college reform was his lead issue. In coordination with his team, TBF channeled its lobbying efforts to meet with every legislator we could. We were able to ensure that the sought-after reforms, as well as additional funding, were both secured within six months after publication of our groundbreaking report. Since then, TBF has awarded an annual prize, named for Governor Patrick, to the community college that collaborates most effectively with employers, a testament to how long a community foundation can stick to an issue beyond political terms of office.

### Affordable Housing (2021)

Housing was always a priority for TBF's public policy work during my tenure. A community foundation can take the long view and stay at the table for many years through many administrations to work on top priority issues. The Boston Foundation has had a long history of supporting CDCs and non-profit housing groups.

Since 2002, the Boston Foundation and the Dukakis Center for Urban and Regional Policy at Northeastern University have produced an annual report called the "Greater Boston Housing Report Card." The report covers the social, political, and economic implications of housing availability, and also addresses the question of housing affordability.

In 2020, the framing of the Report Card shifted to focus on the impact of COVID-19 on housing stability, racial equity and housing, and housing resilience at a moment when the pandemic was believed—hoped?—to be a short-term malady. The next year, the Report Card maintained its focus on the effects of persistent COVID.

In January 2021, just as I was announcing my plans to retire from the Boston Foundation, Governor Charlie Baker approved a $627 million economic impact bill, in part to address a tremendous crisis in the availability of affordable housing. H.5250 included, among other provisions, $50 million for affordable housing near transit hubs, $50 million for neighborhood stabilization to address blighted or vacant housing, and an increase of state Low-Income Housing Tax Credits from $20 to $40 million with no sunset provision.

The final edition of the Greater Boston Housing Report Card during my tenure as CEO, whose annual release had become the signature event in the housing policy world of Massachusetts, landed firmly on the necessary zoning reforms that Governor Baker would champion for the remainder of his second term. TBF had not only provided the intellectual ammunition, but also the center of gravity to move progressive housing policy forward.

## Public-Private Partnerships

By the time I joined the Boston Foundation, I had amassed nearly three decades of experience using the model of public-private partnerships to address big issues that no one sector could tackle alone. I saw no reason to abandon that tried-and-true strategy in my new 21st century work. All of our

Paul Grogan, accompanied by TBF's Bob Wadsworth, visiting a new pilot school, circa 2010. *Courtesy of the Boston Foundation.*

public policy work was structured this way. We applied it to our growing portfolio of education and employment initiatives as well.

One of our early studies (2003) was a rather negative critique of the public workforce system. In response, TBF created a Workforce Solutions Group which resulted in the creation of SkillWorks at the Foundation. Skill-Works is a nationally recognized regional workforce collaborative launched by the Boston Foundation with the Private Industry Council and Boston Public Schools. We mobilized other foundations to make it happen. Philanthropy, government, community organizations, and employers work together to help low-skill, low-income individuals secure family-supporting jobs, and help employers find and retain employers. Today, SkillWorks is considered a model for cities across the country and for the National Fund for Workforce Solutions.

Success Boston is a citywide college completion initiative. It was launched in 2008 in response to a longitudinal study (starting with 1985

Dr. Charles Desmond, former chairman of the Massachusetts Board of Higher Education, and Paul Grogan. *Courtesy of the Boston Foundation.*

(Left to right) Paul Grogan, Mayor Tom Menino, Police Commissioner Paul Evans, and Rev. Dr. Ray Hammond. *Courtesy of the Boston Foundation.*

data) conducted by Northeastern University's Center for Labor Market studies using the National Student Clearinghouse database. The Boston Foundation funded this research published in a report called *Getting to the Finish Line*. The study showed that only 35% of Boston students who enrolled in college completed either an associate or bachelor's degree by the time they turned twenty-five. Enrollment rates were increasing, but completion rates were not.

With the success of a workforce initiative in our pockets, PIC Executive Director Neil Sullivan and I met with then-Mayor Tom Menino to share the bad news. We had a $5 million pledge in hand to soften the blow. The purpose of the grant was to hire coaches to work directly with students to help them make the transition from high school to local colleges.

> "Boston is ready for a revolution, ready to fire an education shot heard round the world, create an opportunity pipeline, and move from incremental to positively disruptive exponential change. That's the goal of the Boston Opportunity Agenda, and in collaboration with partners, we can make that goal a reality."
>
> —Rev. Dr. Ray Hammond, founding chair, Boston Opportunity Agenda

Three key partners—the Boston Foundation, Boston Public Schools (BPS), and the City of Boston—worked with thirty-seven area institutions of higher education, led by UMass Boston and Bunker Hill Community College, as well as local nonprofit partners. The goal was to double the college completion rate for BPS students from 35% to 70%. By 2019, the result had increased to 63%, but dropped back to 52% two years later as a direct result of the pandemic.[9] Success Boston is now a program of the Boston Opportunity Agenda.

The Boston Opportunity Agenda (BOA) is a public/private partnership created in 2011 to focus on educational equity: dramatically increase the pace and scale of student success for all children in Boston attending public, charter, and Catholic schools. BOA is housed at the Boston Foundation and is a member of the national StriveTogether network. It is governed by the CEOs of 16 partner organizations.

BOA focuses on the entire educational pipeline, from birth to career. Scores of organizations work in collaboration on early literacy and reading proficiency; access to high level mathematics; summer learning academies; proficiency in the Massachusetts Comprehensive Assessment System (MCAS); high school completion; high school redesign; and post-secondary attainment including education and employment pathways. Summarizing the breadth and depth of BOA partners and goals would necessitate its own report card (which is available, separately), but suffice to say that this collaborative and comprehensive pipeline approach has generated positive results for Boston students beyond what any one partner could achieve alone.

(Left to right) Mike Durkin, former CEO of United Way of Massachusetts Bay; Elizabeth Pauley, former TBF Senior Program Officer; Barry Shrage, former president of Combined Jewish Philanthropies; Paul Grogan; Mayor Tom Menino; and Rev. Ray Hammond, former chair of the Boston Foundation. *Courtesy of the Boston Foundation.*

## Shaping a Sector: Transforming the Field of Community Foundations

We did not set out to create a national model for community foundations. We tried to create something that would impact Boston and the Boston Foundation. We kept our heads down and did the work. There was no campaign to be in the national spotlight or deliver civic leadership strategies to the field. The national replication happened very organically.

The larger community foundations—roughly the top thirty-five in the country—meet annually to discuss a variety of internal and contextual issues facing our organizations. As colleagues began to hear about our work in Boston, we were invited to make presentations to this group of CEOs and

> Paul has created a new vision of philanthropy, not just for the Boston Foundation, but for community foundations across the country.
>
> —Sandra Edgerley, former chair, the Boston Foundation

board chairs. Soon we were hosting other foundations in Boston to share our vision and approach.

The question was how to inject our sector more fully into the larger ambitions of the time. It's absolutely stunning to me how the imperative of community leadership caught on.

Many national foundations did not really see community foundations as platforms for innovation. Too many community foundations had turned into

Paul Grogan speaking to community foundation CEOs at an Executive Leadership Institute. *Courtesy of CFLeads. Photo by John Altdorfer.*

Paul Grogan with Shelly O'Quinn, CEO of the Innovia Foundation in Spokane, Washington. *Courtesy of CFLeads.*

check-writing bureaucracies for donor advised funds. My view was that we had to shake up community foundations from within. The world has changed, and we should be leading rather than following the change process.

Since 2013, the nonprofit CFLeads[10] has carried forward the imperative to move the whole sector of community foundations forward. Rightly or wrongly, I get a lot of credit for having stimulated this, set it in motion, and most importantly, provided an example of what we have done in Boston that has captured the imagination of a lot of folks.

In 2019, CFLeads commissioned research and issued a report called "Igniting the Future of Community Foundations" to take stock of the scope and scale of civic leadership across the country. What they found is that 98% of community foundations planned to expand or deepen their community leadership work over the next few years, demonstrating sector-wide recognition of the importance of taking on a community leadership role.

The report concluded that "bringing the community together to discuss common challenges has been a core function of community foundations for some time." Influencing public policy matters increasingly. Community foundations recognize that the challenges their communities face are too large to be solved by any one organization or sector alone. It is no longer a boutique function to fund policy advocacy or speak out about specific public policy issues. In a surprising result, 30% of community foundations said they gained more donors than they lost as a result of their policy work, and even more said they plan to devote more staff resources to public policy.

## Closing Thoughts on the Boston Foundation: An Extraordinary Career Capstone

Occasionally it was better to be lucky than good. We worked on hot button issues and had much more impact than we ever thought we could. We got almost no blowback on anything we did, except from unions (on education). But from the general community, what I remember is just a ton of "attaboys" from everybody that the Boston Foundation is alive and kicking. There was a lot of validation of our new approach.

The Boston Foundation's commitment to civic leadership has become deeply ingrained in the fabric of the institution and its quest to create opportunity and equity for all. I am deeply humbled by the fact that the 2022 strategic plan developed by my successor, M. Lee Pelton, is built on the idea that "civic leadership is the most powerful way to advance equity in Greater Boston" and that "collecting data and commissioning research, convening conversations, and using our shared knowledge to work with others to advocate for systems change" is central to the Foundation's work.

"Boston is wonderfully, dynamically, alive. And it is alive above all else because this city understood how to restore and replenish what is special and distinctive about the urban experience. The comeback of Boston was anything but natural—against all odds and unforeseen. The truly wonderful thing is that it was engineered—by politicians, business leaders, and community activists who stubbornly refused to accept the apparent verdict of history on Boston. Do you want to know why I'm an optimist about Boston? Because that [resident] activism is an inexhaustible resource. It will guide us—and save us—in the very interesting days ahead."[11]

*Retirement Party Toast by Ira Jackson (2021)*

I've had the good fortune to have been on the selection committee that gave Paul both his first and last jobs.

When I was Mayor Kevin White's Chief of Staff, I hired Paul straight out of Williams College. I had so much confidence in Paul's ability that I resigned shortly after he arrived.

Twenty-six years later, I was also on the selection committee that chose Paul to lead the Boston Foundation and take us into a new era of civic leadership.

The one concern we had was that Paul might someday run for mayor himself.

Little did we know that Paul would serve longer as CEO of TBF than Tom Menino served as Mayor, and in the process became something perhaps more important: the conscience of the city.

I've known and respected Paul for forty-six years. Perhaps someone might say that I was his sponsor, or maybe even a mentor. The truth is that Paul became my teacher, and that he exceeded every expectation that I and others had in him at every step of his career.

Paul, you are simply remarkable and admirable. What you've done for the Boston Foundation is what we asked of you and more. Like a good citizen of Athens, you took your oath of service and citizenship seriously and left us stronger, wiser, healthier than when you found us. I toast you for being a good steward, and for making all of us who have had the privilege to call you a colleague and a friend, and this city that you love, better.

# — 8 —

# Be Prepared
# to Be Lucky

I hope by this point I have interested you, my reader, in considering a career (or volunteering) in the civic life of your community.

I came to Boston from a fairly sheltered small-town existence and went to a private college in Western Massachusetts. I thought that period of my life was the high-water mark, defining my ideas about how things had to work. But I really got turned around, not in a specific political direction—more conservative or more liberal. Rather, I was convinced to pursue a career as a civic leader by how wonderfully complicated and full of contradictions everything is in a big city. Every notion I had when I arrived in Boston was utterly confounded by the reality of events in a way that I now regard as a very rich experience.

*Be Prepared to Be Lucky* firmly establishes that things can get better in any city as a result of the ambition to make things better. Boston is just one example of a city that has improved dramatically. But Boston's success is fragile and has been squandered before. Although some social and economic issues have been resolved, and others remain unchanged, new issues have emerged in cities (and rural areas) across the nation that will require great intentionality to address.

On the heels of an unmistakable urban renaissance, with Boston as but one example, serious challenges remain for this next generation. While its parameters may change over time, affordable housing remains a persistent problem. Growing concerns about climate change—how it affects the health and well-being of low-income communities—are escalating in ways not previously imagined. Crises of racial equity have escalated, exposing even greater depths of disparity. There is much to be done to achieve peaceful equilibrium between celebrating real progress and accepting the weight of new challenges.

Inspiring new solutions to intractable problems, transforming traditional institutions, and inventing new forms of cooperation, is a wonderfully American phenomenon. As Boston Mayor Kevin White once said, one must be defiantly optimistic. If we lose our American cities, we also lose the vision of a better future for the generations that follow us.

We need to protect and preserve our democracy. My ten years serving in city government showed me that determined, creative, and collaborative leadership can turn a city back from the brink. My experience opened doors for me that I could never have imagined possible. I encourage young people to set aside doubtful cynicism and enter a public service career or participate in civic life as a volunteer.

My good friend Micho Spring, with whom I worked at the City of Boston and who later joined the Board of the Boston Foundation, confirms my sense that what I learned during a decade working for city government became the through-line of my entire career:

> Paul focused on what he cared about, the issues that were important to him, and he was able to maintain that intentional focus through all of his jobs. He also understood the need to weave policy and politics together in order to succeed. It's rare when people can do that, but in today's world, you need to have political acumen to be able to tackle complex issues with all your skills, intentionality, and intensity.

Real progress will depend on a steady stream of talented, bright, and idealistic people coming into government and nonprofit organizations, and believing that those sectors are wonderful places to exercise their faculties and views. My own experience in government and nonprofits says to me that this is quite possible.

As the baby boom generation retires, today's young people will have a surprisingly large role to play in continuing the urban renaissance. As I discovered through my own experience, if you hang around at a government job long enough, you get asked to take on leadership roles that may go beyond your qualifications on paper. People are coming and going all the time, so young people get to exercise an extraordinary amount of responsibility. Bright young people bring new ideas and innovation, both necessary for cities to evolve and thrive. This rewarding experience is very hard to replicate in the private sector.

Government is still one of the best and most effective places to exercise one's idealism and one's concern for the overall character and prospects of American life. We should also have confidence in the reliability and results of the nonprofit sector to make a difference.

And while the actions—or inactions—of government occasionally give us pause, the public sector remains the biggest investor in community development and the well-being of low-income neighborhood residents. The reality of working in government is that one of its central virtues is also one of the most vexing things about it. What I mean by that is there is no fixed bottom line for the performance of government, or for that matter in the nonprofit sector, and therefore no bottom line for you or the performance of any individual within the organization. The shifting currents in political life are certainly maddening! The nature of the work creates a struggle to stay focused. I find that exhilarating because it is real life. I don't think there is anything quite like it.

Without knowing exactly what will happen as a result, I believe it is time to renew the nation's quest to tap young people who are willing to commit at least a portion of their careers to work in government and nonprofit organizations. We should actively invite young people to step up to the next generation of civic leadership, to be adroit "boundary crossers" with credibility and standing in diverse communities and multiple sectors.

For all of you considering a career in government or the civic sector, there are so many unresolved and new issues to take on. Focus on what you care about and take it from there. Today's issues are complicated. Making a difference requires deep integration within communities. It's like playing without a net. The profile of civic leaders fits more neatly into this environment—more so than political or business leaders—and they can potentially accomplish much more.

For those who aspire to spend at least a portion of their careers in the private sector, you can count on the fact that the kinds of skills, talents, and experiences developed while working in government and nonprofit organizations are increasingly prized by private employers. The walls have really come down between the public and private worlds. It's a very good time for people who come into public service to be a little bit more relaxed about enjoying a public career of some duration, knowing that they can move on to whatever they might like to do next in their careers.

In closing this chapter and memoir, I want to share three abiding thoughts and pieces of advice that have served me well over the years. I had the honor of delivering the commencement speech in 2018 to graduates of Suffolk University (MA) Sawyer Business School. I stand by the advice and encouragement I gave to graduates to consider career avenues in public service:

> *Be unreasonable.* In 1903, George Bernard Shaw wrote that the reasonable man adapts himself to the world. The unreasonable man persists in trying to adapt the world to himself. Therefore, all progress depends on the unreasonable man. Why is this so? Well, powerful interests conspire to keep things the way they are. They are fiercely resistant to change, because they benefit from the status quo. Some of you are graduating with degrees in public administration and going into public service, and you'll have your encounters with large, unresponsive bureaucracies, and a failure to confront the real problems we have. Housing is a great example. The reality is, there's no way for cities to meet the housing crisis without dramatically increasing density in

BE PREPARED TO BE LUCKY

neighborhoods that have long been accustomed only to single family homes. We're going to need courageous public servants who can stand up to this pressure, and citizen activists who can slowly reshape public opinion in their communities toward progress.

*Don't let economic success be the extent of your ambition.* The famed New York Yankees catcher and manager, Yogi Berra, once said, "I don't make predictions, especially about the future." But I'm willing to forecast a lot of economic success for this group of graduates. Many of you will make excellent livings, and a good living in America puts you at the top of the world food chain. Some of you will have the opportunity to make enormous amounts of money. And don't get me wrong, I think that's great. There's no doubt that the prospect of personal reward in this economy creates much of the dynamism and success and entrepreneurship we enjoy. But there's just too much wisdom that says material success is not enough to satisfy the soul. I can't tell you how many successful people I know who arrive in late middle age with a sinking feeling that they haven't made a difference in people's lives. So I implore you to volunteer, to vote, to donate to charity. But moreover, be an active citizen, and fight on behalf of your fellow neighbors who don't enjoy the full promise of American life.

*Be prepared to be lucky.* E.B. White, the famed essayist and author of *Charlotte's Web,* offered it as advice to a young man who was about to move to New York City in 1949. The full quote is "no one should come to New York to live unless he is willing to be lucky." But I think my adaptation applies to all of us, not just those headed to the Big Apple. There's a perennial argument among philosophers as to whether human beings make their own lives, or rather are in the grip of forces beyond our control. Are we captains of our fate? Or mere pawns on a chess board? E.B. White doesn't resolve this for us, but rather acknowledges the likelihood that whatever happens is the result of the interplay between what we do and what is done to us. And, moreover, that expecting the best probably enhances your prospects.

Be willing to be unreasonable, don't let economic success define the limit of your ambitions, and most of all, be prepared to be lucky. I wish you great success in your own civic leadership journey!

# Impact by the Numbers

## "THE TRANSFORMATION OF THE BOSTON FOUNDATION: A LEGACY OF LEADERSHIP"

### 2001-2021

**TWO DECADES OF EXPONENTIAL
FINANCIAL GROWTH:**

**$1.7**

billion in assets. Total assets
more than doubled.

**$28**

million in unrestricted
funds raised for the Campaign
for Civic Leadership.

**$1.9**

billion in grants. This represents 83%
of all grants since 1915.

**$914**

million in donor advised
fund assets (up from
$184 million in 2001).

---

**CIVIC LEADERSHIP STRATEGY:**

**240**

research reports

**410**

public forums and
webinars

Over **41,000**

people attended forums
and webinars

Announcing $250 million "Race to the Top" grant award at the Massachusetts State House.
*Courtesy of the Boston Foundation.*

---

### COMMUNITY IMPACT:

*Education:*

**$20**

million increase in state funds for
community colleges

**$250**

million in federal Race to the Top
funds leveraged through K-12
education reform impacting
700,000 students

**77%**

increase in college completion since
Success Boston launched

*Housing and neighborhoods:*

**$8.5**

million Program Related Investments
(PRIs) for affordable housing

**$20**

million in grants strengthening
transportation and infrastructure in
the Fairmount Corridor

**22,769**

homes built by CDCs since 2001

Photo continued.

---

*Workforce development:*

## $132

million for workforce
development leveraged by
SkillWorks since 2003

## $384

million invested in the National
Fund for Workforce Development,
modeled on SkillWorks

## $5.2

million invested in 16 Black and
Latinx owned businesses since
2018 through the Business
Equity Fund

*Arts and culture:*

## 98%

of K-8 students receiving arts
education in Boston Public
Schools through EdVestors

## $3

million from Live Arts Boston
to artists; 77% artists of color

*Health care:*

## $15

million raised to help
those most affected by the
COVID-19 pandemic

# Interviews

Thank you to these individuals who so generously gave their time to share reflections on the intersections of their lives with Paul Grogan's career. While each person has an extensive and impressive biography, we have limited this summary to current career descriptions and, *in italics*, each person's primary link to Paul's career.

**Stephen Chan**
Senior Advisor for Partnerships, City of Boston Mayor's Office
*The Boston Foundation*

**Andy Ditton**
Former LISC executive and retired Citi managing director; Adjunct Professor, Columbia University School of International and Public Affairs
*LISC*

**Mayor Ray Flynn**
Former Boston mayor
1984–1993 (retired)
*City of Boston*

**Patty Foley**
President, Save the Harbor/Save the Bay (retired)
*LISC, The Boston Foundation*

**Ellen Gilligan**
President & CEO, The Greater Milwaukee Foundation
*LISC, The Boston Foundation*

**Carol Glazer**
President, National Organization on Disability
*LISC*

**Peter Goldmark**
President of the Rockefeller Foundation, and chairman and CEO of the *International Herald Tribune* (retired)
*LISC*

**Joe Hagan**
President, National Equity Fund (retired)
*LISC*

**Rev. Dr. Ray Hammond**
Co-founder and Pastor, Bethel AME
Church in Boston
*The Boston Foundation*

**Tom Howley**
Senior Vice President,
Howley Bread Group
*City of Boston*

**Alberto Ibargüen**
CEO, The John S. and James L.
Knight Foundation
*Harvard, The Boston Foundation*

**Ira Jackson**
Research Fellow, Harvard Kennedy School
Mossavar-Rahmani Center for Business
and Government
*City of Boston, The Boston Foundation*

**Robert Lewis, Jr.**
President & CEO, Boys and Girls
Clubs of Boston
*The Boston Foundation*

**Ed Lloyd**
CFO and COO, US Fund for UNICEF
(retired)
*LISC*

**Jake Mascotte**
President & CEO, Blue Cross Blue Shield
Kansas City (retired)
*LISC*

**Travis McCready**
Head of Life Sciences, Industries Americas
JLL
*Harvard, The Boston Foundation*

**Mary Jo Meisner**
President, MJM Advisory Services
*The Boston Foundation*

**Governor Deval Patrick**
Co-Director and Professor of Practice,
Harvard Kennedy School Center
for Public Leadership
*The Boston Foundation*

**Vanessa Calderón-Rosado**
CEO, Inquilinos Boricuas en Acción (IBA)
*The Boston Foundation*

**Michael Rubinger**
President & CEO, LISC (retired)
*LISC*

**R. T. Rybak**
The Minneapolis Foundation
*The Boston Foundation*

**Marvin Siflinger**
HUD Regional Director (retired)
*City of Boston*

**Micho Spring**
Chief Reputation Officer, Weber
Shandwick (retired)
*City of Boston, The Boston Foundation*

**David Stanley**
CEO, Payless Cashways (retired)
*LISC*

**Neil Sullivan**
Executive Director, Boston Private
Industry Council
*City of Boston*

## Michael Taylor
President, Urban College
of Boston (retired)
*City of Boston*

## Darren Walker
President, The Ford Foundation
*LISC, The Boston Foundation*

# Acknowledgments

With gratitude, we thank the following individuals for sponsoring the creation of this book. Their generosity makes it possible for 100% of all book sales to benefit the civic leadership work of the Boston Foundation.

Bill Barke

Rick Burnes

Jim Canales and Jim McCann

The Connors Family

Brian and Karen Conway

Dick DeWolf

Sandy and Paul Edgerley

Michael and Barbara Eisenson

Grace and Ted Fey

Joel Fleishman

Bob and Diane Hildreth

Barbara and Amos Hostetter

Martha and Michael Keating

The John S. and James L. Knight Foundation

Jack Meyer

Thank you to Bill Barke, former executive chairman of Pearson's North American Higher Education Group and president of Allyn & Bacon, for his wise editorial guidance in shaping the final manuscript.

A special thank you to the staff of the Boston Foundation:

- M. Lee Pelton, President and CEO, for his enthusiastic support of the book project.
- Al Van Ranst, Jr., Chief Financial Officer, and his finance team for overseeing the book project.
- Barbara Hindley, Associate Vice President, Communications, for her review of Chapters 6 and 7 to ensure historical accuracy, and for collecting photos from the Foundation's archives.
- Keith Mahoney, Vice President for Communications and Public Affairs, for amplifying stories of public policy wins in Chapter 7.
- Kate Guedj, Vice President for Development, and her team for helping to manage book sponsorship gifts.

# Glossary

| | |
|---|---|
| BHP | Boston Housing Partnership |
| BOA | Boston Opportunity Agenda |
| BPS | Boston Public Schools |
| CDC | Community Development Corporation |
| CDT | Community Development Trust |
| DAF | Donor Advised Fund |
| HUD | Housing and Urban Development (federal agency) |
| HUDC | Harlem Urban Development Corporation |
| LIHTC | Low Income Housing Tax Credit |
| LIMAC | Local Initiatives Managed Asset Corporation |
| LISC | Local Initiatives Support Corporation |
| NCDI | National Community Development Initiative |
| NDEA | Neighborhood Development & Employment Agency (Boston) |
| NDSC | Neighborhood Development Support Collaborative |
| NEF | National Equity Fund |
| PIC | Private Industry Council |
| PILOT | Payment in Lieu of Taxes |
| REIT | Real Estate Investment Trust |
| TBF | The Boston Foundation |

# References

The Boston Foundation. "The Transformation of The Boston Foundation: A Legacy of
Leadership by Paul S. Grogan, President and CEO, 2001-2021."

*Boston Globe Editorial.* "What Harvard Owes to Allston." August 25, 1999.

*Boston Globe Editorial.* "Stepping to the Plate." April 2, 2002.

CFLeads. "Going All-In on Community Leadership: Igniting the Future of Community
Foundations." 2019.

Daniel P. Dain. "Boston's Future depends on whether we remember lessons from the
past." *Boston Globe.* August 27, 2023.

Anthony DePalma. "Tax Credits Produce Housing for Poor." *New York Times.* January 17,
1988.

https://forwardcities.org/about/our-story/

Michael K. Frisby. "Hub neighborhoods ask: After Grogan, what?" *Boston Globe.*
November 19, 1985.

Ben Gose. "A Boston Fund Mixes Research and Advocacy with Writing Checks." *Chronicle
of Philanthropy.* Volume XXIII, No. 14. June 2, 2011.

Zoe Greenberg. "Paul Grogan to Step Down from Boston Foundation. *Boston Globe.*
January 28, 2020.

Paul Grogan. "Proof Positive: A Community-based Solution to America's Affordable
Housing Crisis." *Stanford Law and Policy Review:* Volume 7:2. September 30, 1996.

Paul Grogan. "Boston is a world-class city, but not an equitable one." Boston Globe
Opinion. May 25, 2021.

Paul S. Grogan. Duke Essays in Contemporary Philanthropy #2: "Changing the Game:
Civic Leadership at The Boston Foundation, 2001-2012." Duke University Sanford
School of Public Policy, Center for Strategic Philanthropy and Civic Society. 2013.

Paul S. Grogan. "Cleveland Urban League Speech" delivered by Mayor Kevin H. White.
Courtesy of Boston City Archives, Box 122, Folder 38.

Paul S. Grogan and Tony Proscio. *Comeback Cities: A Blueprint for Urban Neighborhood Revival.*
Westview Press: 2000.

Emily Hiestand and Ande Zellman, editors. *The Good City: Writers Explore 21ˢᵗ Century Boston.* Beacon Press, 2004. Excerpts from the Introduction by Paul Grogan.

Bob Herbert. Op-Ed "In America." *The New York Times.* December 28, 2000.

Alexander von Hoffman. *House by House, Block by Block: The Rebirth of America's Urban Neighborhoods.* Oxford University Press, 2003.

David Holmstrom. "Help and Hope for the Inner City." *The Christian Science Monitor.* August 25, 1994.

Howard Husock. "A Compact for Boston's Hard Work High." *New York Times Archives.* April 10, 1988.

Ira A. Jackson. "The great Boston comeback story." *Boston Globe Opinion.* November 2, 2017.

Lynn Jenkins. "Don't Just Give. Solve. The Boston Foundation Embraces Innovation and Constant Learning in Pursuit of Educational Equity." Grantmakers for Education: Case Study No. 17: Principles for Effective Grantmaking. September 2017.

Joseph P. Kahn. "Man About Town: Paul Grogan prepares to take over the Boston Foundation." *Boston Globe.* June 5, 2001.

Thomas M. Keane, Jr. "Foundation vaults into hub prominence." *Boston Herald.* May 27, 2004.

Jeffrey Marshall. "A Redevelopment Pioneer Reflects." *US Banker.* February 1999.

Deanna Pan. "45 Years Ago Black Protesters Sought to Desegregate Carson Beach." *Boston Globe.* July 13, 2020.

Lisa Pierpont. "Hedging his funds." *Boston Common-Magazine.com.* circa 2015.

Charles A. Radin. "United Way pledges $1.8 million for housing." *Boston Globe.* March 18, 1987.

Ron Stodghill. *Business Week.* "Bringing Hope Back to the 'Hood." August 19, 1996.

Mitchell Sviridoff. "The Seeds of Urban Revival." *The Public Interest.* New York: Winter 1994, pp. 82-103.

Joan Vennochi. "Added duty for Hub neighborhood chief: He'll become business liaison for Flynn." *Boston Globe.* March 26, 1985.

Williams College Archives and Special Collections: Oral History Project. Interviewer Charles R. Alberti. January 8, 2003.

# Endnotes

## Chapter 1

1   *The Good City: Writers Explore 21st Century Boston.* Introduction by Paul Grogan.

2   *The Good City.* Introduction by Paul Grogan.

3   "Cleveland Urban League Speech," February 14, 1976. Written by Paul S. Grogan, delivered by Mayor Kevin H. White. Courtesy of Boston City Archives, Box 122, Folder 38.

## Chapter 2

4   The term "white hat" came from early Western movies in which the good guys wore white or light-colored hats.

## Chapter 3

5   Nonprofit Metrics LLC. "Cause IQ. Directory of Nonprofits: Community Development Corporations." © 2023.

## Chapter 4

6   William and Flora Hewlett Foundation, John S. and James L. Knight Foundation, Lilly Endowment, John D. and Catherine T. MacArthur Foundation, Pew Charitable Trusts, Surdna Foundation, and Prudential Insurance Company.

## Chapter 5

7   *The Good City.* Introduction by Paul Grogan.

## Chapter 6

8   The Vault was the nickname for the Coordinating Committee, a quasi-secret organization created in 1959 by Boston's business elite. Born out of frustration with a corrupt and inept city government, in the early days, its members helped elect mayors and guide Boston's renaissance.

**Chapter 7**

9  WBUR. "New Report finds setbacks in college enrollment and completion rates for Boston Public Schools graduates." March 23, 2023.

10  CFLeads was established in 1994 as the National Coalition of Community Foundations for Youth, a supporting organization of The Greater Kansas City Community Foundation. The organization became CFLeads (Community Foundations Leading Change) in 2013 and became an independent entity in 2017.

11  *The Good City*. Introduction by Paul Grogan.

# Index

busing, 4, 9-10, 12, 15-16, 21-22
Butts, Calvin, 45, 80-82

**C**
Calderon-Rosado, Vanessa, 28, 113, 120
Cambridge Affordable Housing Trust, 95
Campaign for Communities, 60
Carey, John, 76
Carson Beach, 12-13, *14*, 15, 87-88, *89*
Carter, Jimmy, 39
The Case for Community Colleges, TBF
    report, 134
CEOs for Cities, 101-102
CETA, 33
CFLeads, 142-144
Chan, Stephen, 121, 128
Charles River, 7, 109
*Charlotte's Web* (White), 151
Chicago, 52-54, 56, 60, 65-66, 72, 82-83,
    98, 101
Chicago Equity Fund, 53, 68
*Christian Science Monitor,* 34
*Chronicle of Philanthropy*, 122-123
City Hall Plaza, 7
City Year, 118
Civic Leadership Fund, 125-127
Civil Rights Movement, xvii
Clinton, Bill, 23, *67-68*, *73*
Clinton, Hillary, *68*
Cogsville, Donald, 80
Collins, John, 7
*Comeback Cities*, xi-xii, xix, 96-98
Combined Jewish Philanthropies, 141
Common Cause, 121
Commonwealth Shakespeare Company, 114
Community Builders, 35, 114
Community Colleges, 134-135, 140, 154
Community Development Block Grant
    programs, 32-33, 40

Community Development Corporations
    (CDC), 33-36, 40-41, 44, 46-49, 52, 55,
    57, 59, 65, 68, 78-83, 87, 120, 135, 154
Community Development Financial
    Institution (CDFI) Act, 84
Community Development Trust (CDT),
    73-75, 84, 96
Community Reinvestment Act, 39
Continental Corporation, *50*, 70
COVID-19, 136, 155
Culpepper, Miniard, 88
Cultural Facilities Act (2006), 128-129
Culture is Our Common Wealth, TBF
    report, 129
Curley, Michael, 7

**D**
Daley, Richard M., 53, *54*, 66, *83*, 101-102
DeLeo, Robert, 133-134
Department of Housing and Urban
    Development (HUD), 32-33, 36-37,
    78, 94, 158
desegregation, 3, 8, 12-13, 16-17, 19-21, 37
Desmond, Charles, *138*
Development Impact Project, 12
Distinguished Bostonian awards
    program, 44
Ditton, Andy, 52-53, 58, 61, 68, 77, 157
Donor Advised Fund (DAF), 115-116
Dukakis, Michael, *24*
Dukakis Center for Urban and Regional
    Policy, 136
Duke University Sanford School of
    Public Policy, Center for Strategic
    Philanthropy and Civil Society, 123
Durbin, Dick, *54*
Durkin, Mike, *141*

170